Ezekiel's Wheel

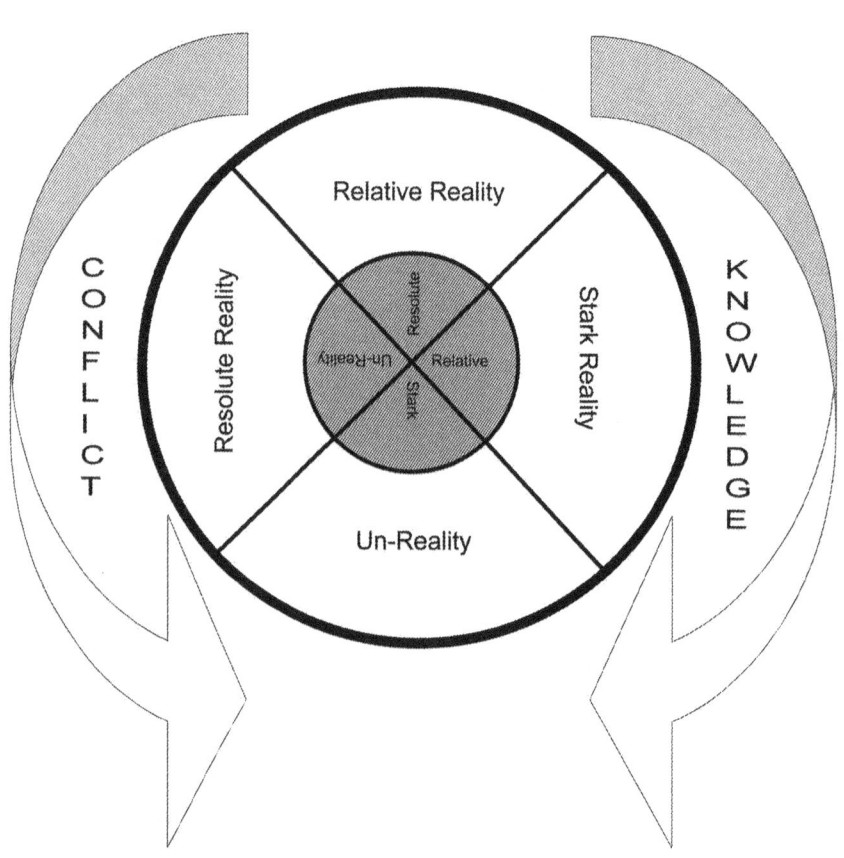

Ezekiel's Wheel

a clear explanation for the human struggle

Connie J. Allen

Writers Club Press
San Jose New York Lincoln Shanghai

Ezekiel's Wheel
a clear explanation for the human struggle

Writers Club Press
an imprint of iUniverse, Inc.

For information address:
iUniverse, Inc.
5220 S. 16th St., Suite 200
Lincoln, NE 68512
www.iuniverse.com

Part one of this book is an illustration, a work of fiction. Names, characters, places and incidents either are products of the author's imagination or are used fictitiously. Any resemblance to actual events or locales or persons, living or dead, is entirely coincidental.

ISBN: 0-595-21617-X

Printed in the United States of America

Dedication

To Bruce,
whose questions and answers helped to steer this research.

To Lauren and Thaddeus,
who gave me the best reason to continue it.

Acknowledgements

Dianne White, my editor and friend, whose sage advice I value more than she knows.

Nita Cosby, my clairvoyant friend without whose personal library, this book would have been incomplete.

Bantam Books, a division of Random House, Inc., for their kind permission to quote Stephen Hawking, A Brief History of Time, 1998.

My indebtedness to others is acknowledged in the Select Bibliography, upon the contents of which I have been so largely dependent.

Please register your comments and questions about this construct through electronic mail at info@callen&associates.com

Ezekiel 1:4–28

I looked, and I saw a windstorm coming out of the north—an immense cloud with flashing lightning and surrounded by brilliant light. The center of the fire looked like glowing metal, and in the fire was what looked like four living creatures. In appearance, their form was that of a man, but each of them had four faces and four wings. Their legs were straight; their feet were like those of a calf and gleamed like burnished bronze. Under their wings on their four sides, they had the hands of a man. All four of them had faces and wings, and their wings touched one another. Each one went straight ahead; they did not turn as they moved.

Their faces looked like this: Each of the four had the face of a man, and on the right side each had the face of a lion, and on the left was the face of an ox; each also had the face of an eagle. Such were their faces. Their wings were spread out upward; each had two wings, one touching the wing of another creature on either side, and two wings covering its body. Each one went straight ahead. Wherever the spirit would go, they would go, without turning as they went. The appearance of the creatures was like burning coals of fire or like torches. Fire moved back and forth among the creatures; it was bright, and lightning flashed out of it. The creatures sped back and forth like flashes of lightning.

As I looked at the living creatures, I saw a wheel on the ground beside each creature with its four faces. This was the appearance and structure of the wheels: they sparkled like chrysolite, and all four looked alike. Each appeared to be made like a wheel intersecting a wheel. As they moved, they would go in any one of the four directions the creatures faced; the wheels did not turn about as the creatures went. Their rims were high and awesome, and all four rims were full of eyes all around.

When the living creatures moved, the wheels beside them moved; and when the living creatures rose from the ground, the wheels also rose. Wherever the spirit would go, they would go, and the wheels would rise along with them, because the spirit of the living creatures was in the wheels. When the creatures moved, they also moved; when the creatures stood still, they also stood still; and when the creatures rose from the ground, the wheels rose along with them, because the spirit of the living creatures was in the wheels.

Spread out above the heads of the living creatures was what looked like an expanse, sparkling like ice, and awesome. Under the expanse, their wings were stretched out one toward the other, and each had two wings covering its body. When the creatures moved, I heard the sound of their wings, like the roar of rushing waters, like the voice of the Almighty, like the tumult of an army. When they stood still, they lowered their wings.

Then there came a voice from above the expanse over their heads was what looked like a throne of sapphire, and high above on the throne was a figure like that of a man. I saw that from what appeared to be his waist up he looked like glowing metal, as if full of fire, and that from there down he looked like fire; and brilliant light surrounded him. Like the appearance of a rainbow in the clouds on a rainy day, so was the radiance around him.

This was the appearance of the likeness of the glory of the Lord. When I saw it, I fell facedown, and I heard the voice of one speaking.

New International Version

Contents

Preface

First, I must apologize. I assume that there are many who are much more learned on the question than I. And not having the background to make such fantastic statements as I have in this essay, I am taking a great personal risk. I know very well that this discourse will serve as a basis to judge both my character and credibility. If I do a poor job and don't prove my point, my credibility will suffer immensely. On the other hand, if it is written well and clearly understood, but does not meld with the current theological view, my character will be assaulted. Either way, it is a risk I must take.

Of course, it is not my intent to persuade you to my ideals. You will have to decide the truth of this construct based upon your own experience, reasoning ability and feelings about what I am about to tell you. If you can believe what I say is true, in whole or in part, then you will come to understand what I have come to know.

You see, I understand now that mankind is spinning on a predestined course that is difficult to see. Life appears to be random. There is too much environmental interference—paying bills, relationships, just living. And because we cannot easily see the patterns beneath every day life, the course is nearly impossible to change. We accept it as if it cannot be changed. We blame each other for the way things are as it is in our nature to do.

This idea of a predestined course is not a new. The bible predicts end of the world events in Revelations. Christians have been preparing for the end of the world for more than a thousand years. But I am not predicting the end of the world. That's too simple. No, I am trying to stop it—at least that which can be stopped.

In all of human history, there has existed a menace, a persecutor, a tormentor. The fight for freedom is designed to destroy him. And at times, he has been thwarted, subdued, but never eliminated.

After the devastation subsides, while the earth regenerates itself and continues to survive, the menace sits, waiting for the proper season to rise up again. Through trickery and schemes, it snatches a morsel of victory before it is again confronted and forced to lay down the cold steel—but not before death and destruction make their way through one quarter of the earth.

In times of prosperity, the menace is forgotten. He is unconsciously fed by the disappearance of the kind and gentle human being. Competition for domination becomes bitter whether religious or secular. Human thoughtlessness reveals itself through gains and losses, over projected earnings and lay offs, casualties in our heads, casualties of the heart. And with each new era comes new diseases as we rush furiously to eliminate old conditions. The progress we make through technological development will eventually be used for some evil purpose—the extinction of the culpable and innocent alike.

We are aware of these things, but nature must take its course. It is the way we are programmed to spin. We close our eyes and ignore the potential consequences.

This construct, which attempts to answer why, is born therefore from religious tradition, overlaid with physical and psychological evidence. It rests on a bed of scientific theory, which lies beneath a spiritual and social conscience. The method is phenomenological based on surveys, observations, historical events, scientific data and my own experiences, the combination of which has been summed up as truth. Judgment and logical supposition has been used in some cases with the absence of proof. It is the final consolidation of that which I have read, observed, internalized and been blessed with the insight to understand.

A Note of Caution

But first, I must caution you before you begin to examine the data. Begin at the beginning. Each chapter builds upon the previous one. If you begin in the middle, you will not understand my mission and you will undoubtedly disagree.

This book is about all of our true selves; so don't be offended if you catch a glimpse of yourself in this mirror. It is what I know to be the truth. I wrestled with my own fears and doubts as the book was being written and I was afraid, then ashamed.

It is not intended to be offensive to any true believer of God's word or any unbeliever. So if you find the strong force or the weak force rising up in you as you read, keep reading. There is a message waiting for you just beyond the words.

This book is not a manual on how you should live your life, change your ways or raise your children. There are too many conflicting ideals on the shelves today written by people with conflicting realities, perspectives. This book may change your life by increasing your awareness of the constant pattern in the chaos revolving around you.

Finally, this book is not the absolute final word on who we are and why we behave as we do. It is a probability equation—the probability is high that you possess the four-dimensional realities in Ezekiel's wheel. The probability is high that in a flight or fight situation, one of the four forces has taken over and you will not be able to control it. The probability is high that when you are in the midst of a controversy you will find it difficult (if not impossible) to change your course unless you can recognize the signs that precede it. The probability is high that unless you come to terms with the *rise*, you will never be able to control it and we will all continue to spin.

After you read this book, you may want to know 'How can I get off of this wheel?' But you already know the answer. It lies within the question—'Am I willing to change myself or am I content blaming my dilemma on the one behind me?'

Introduction

Why must we struggle against the odds all of our lives?

Ezekiel's Wheel is a thought provoking account of the conflict which exists between human beings. It describes who we are, looks at the biblical evidence and the scientific reasons why we behave, think, say and do what we do. It breaks the code so that we can individually identify the roles we act out and collectively change the cycle that will lead us to the much sought after prize—peace.

This book is both controversial and important, especially now. People are seeking the truth. People are fighting for peace. Parents are losing children and children are growing up without parents. When will that which divides us take its place in the insignificant pile? Triumph can come much sooner than you know. The answer is closer than you expect. It is learning—the first step. Then understanding—the second step, then acceptance—the third step and finally adaptation—the fourth step. The children must be taught this message. They are resilient. They are the ones with the power to change the world.

Haven't you ever wondered why you say the things you say, act the way you act and believe what you believe? The true reason for it is deeper in your psyche than Freud's reality or Jung's clairvoyance. It begins in the beginning with a tale so familiar we no longer hear the words. It begins with the first man and first woman and builds on their story to the present day where the story is still the same—only the scenery has changed.

Each of us is playing a role—one role in the four that were created centuries ago—back in the beginning. These roles are predestined. They will be played out until we destroy each other unless we learn what must be learned to change our collective fate. Right now, we can only see the obvious, superficial world, the world that affects us day to day. These beliefs are rooted so deeply that they are hidden in coded messages. We identify it as our intuitive power. But, it is so much more than this. It is the mystery of life, encoded in our DNA, our genes.

In Ezekiel's Wheel, you will discover who you were before the civilized nations of the world told you who you were supposed to be and dress and act and think and speak. You will come to know why after more than 3000 centuries, Israel and the bordering countries are still at war over land that amounts to a hill of beans, dust. You will come to understand why the "love holidays"—Thanksgiving and Christmas—are dreaded family gatherings instead of the happy reunion that the word "holiday" implies.

External profiling is a simple matter when you have a clear description of the enemy. But, what if your enemy looks just like you on the outside? What if the enemy is your brother, or sister, mother or father, husband or wife? Profiling can point to false leads and possibilities with luck or chance as the deciding factor.

In the true war, the war that lies beneath the chaos of living, within the mystery to all of the madness, there are four who are at war. We find these repeating themselves in Ezekiel's Wheel, in nature, in science, in ourselves. They are a part of the natural cycle of life embedded in our genes. They are, in fact, what drives life, spinning forward toward a destructive end.

Part One is a fable, which illustrates how the four negotiate their way through life alternating between ignoring what is hidden or confronting it. Part Two explains the controversy, clarifies the key terms so that we begin on equal footing and then lays out the construct.

The construct begins with Ezekiel's wheel as described in the bible. Then it shows the truth of his vision by examining the four realities of man—resolute, relative, stark, and finally, unreality. These four realities are how we perceive the world. It then demonstrates those in the past and the present whose births and behaviour fit these four profiles. This construct could not be true without the physical proof discerned through science, so in the next section, the physical evidence is laid out and compared to the biblical evidence. Then undoubtedly, there will be questions—questions of determinism, predestination, freewill, even of God. These are anticipated and answered based on what is written in the bible and documented through scientific methods. The last section brings it all together so that we can make sense of the world, our present state of existence and how we can achieve the much sought after peace prize. It's what we all want, isn't it?

Tables

PART ONE

The Enigma of Mankind

I must tell you this story as I remember it. It is not so long that you will lose interest or so short that you will lose my meaning. But it must be told so that you can remember and pass it on. Although I am sure that you knew it once, I know that it has been hidden in your own daily struggles. I am here to remind you.

And this story is absolutely true.

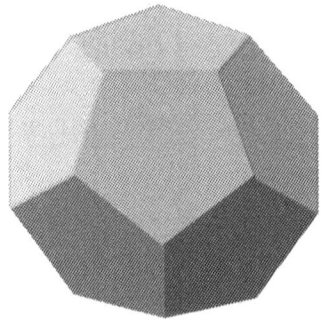

The Natural State of Being

And the father, after being away for some time, feared his increasing loss of influence over his children. And since he had become aware of their lack of commitment to each other, he planned a visit to see for himself the truth of their beliefs. As it had been foretold and documented, he was growing undeniably old and the time had come for him to decide on the type of inheritance he would leave each of them. He had his servant pack enough food and drink to carry him throughout his journey. Then bidding his wife farewell, he headed toward the home of his first-born.

At the end of the first day's journey, he stopped underneath a stout tree to rest and eat the supper that had been prepared for him. He had just laid back his head against the tree trunk and closed his eyes, when an overwhelming urge came over him. He opened his eyes straight away and sat upright as the energy moved through his chest down to his feet. He arose without deliberation and gathered his things for the short journey to his son's house.

Dusk had just settled in to night and if he hurried, he could just make it before the midnight hour. He moved swiftly, past trees, rocks and burial mounds. His cloak brushed up against the low dead branches of the brush as he passed. But he neither saw nor felt the impact of the scrapes. His mind was focused on reaching the first cause before it was too late.

~~

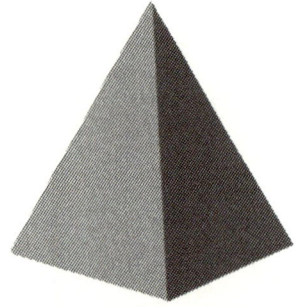

The man Jacob was known to be the *first cause* because he was the first-born but beneath it all, he was really the *weak force*. Now the determination of weak or strong is solely man's convention. So, this designation must be considered in the proper perspective. He was not weak because he was afraid. He had plenty of courage to lead, to choose, to live. He was not physically weak. He was well equipped to lift the fallen tree or shoulder the wood after chopping; nor was he considered weak because he wept inconsolably, he rarely cried at all. There is no glory in tears. He considered them to be a sign of weakness. He was not weak because he was fearful. He was not afraid to take the hard stance or try the patience of the world. No, the man Jacob was weak simply because he was born that way. It was fashioned in his ability to exert his force of will over others. It was molded into his plasma, the basis of his human condition, the extent of his span of control.

Now Jacob's will, in comparison to the other three, was not at all weak. He was clever and knew instinctively how to manipulate the world to fulfill his needs. During his long life, he introduced—even accelerated—all manner of decay of the human spirit with the force of his words—suggestions really. And, in his idealistic world, his actions were required, justified and necessary. He believed he was the way.

He came from the east, born prematurely, the first in the set of the unexpected three who were rocked from inside his mother's womb. When the first was born, she gave him the name Jacob. He was beautiful with brown sugar skin and tight black locks that fell across his fine forehead. She smiled and held him tightly to her breast and cradled him gently in her arms as he wailed aloud for life.

His mother's joy did not last long. Her smile turned to searing pain as she felt her insides turning over for a second time. She looked and saw another just like the first and she was frightened when she saw him. She clutched him close to her heart and called his name—Oh, Fear.

Within moments of the second, she felt the pain of childbirth for the third time and cried out bitterly at the sight of the small and wretched, deformed ball of clay as he delivered onto the rich earth. She called his name—Ah, Bitterness. And these two would live in Jacob's shadow all of his life.

After the commotion of his birth and the after birth of his brothers was forgotten, Jacob opened his large brown eyes for twelve seconds to scope out the lay of the land. He found that it was not safe for him. He shut his eyes again tightly for twelve days and waited, wailing continually as those around him scrambled to meet his needs, to calm his desire, to suppress the rise. He controlled the world. And everyone waited for him.

On the twelfth day, he opened his eyes just a tiny bit to see what the world had in store. He was met with cheers of surprise and greeted by a throng of neighbors and well-wishers. And he was pleased. And everyone who saw him said 'what a great man he will be, so beautiful. He is good'.

As a child, Jacob was good, sweet and caring, seeking his mother's favor though good deeds and earning her praise with works. He was always the first to volunteer, to help when the others would not. His mother rewarded him with the sweet or the hug or the kiss on the cheek. His smile broadened with her approval. And he adored her.

On occasion, being the human child that he was and imperfect, he erred. But the consequences of imperfection killed his spirit and were too bitter a pill to swallow. And there was the guilt. So, he resorted to small lies, harmless and unimportant. And to his amazement, there was no disruption, no change, no consequences. His mother kept smiling and did not correct him. Then he reasoned through his own logical mind that he must do *this* for her. He did not want her to be unhappy. She was very important to him. He needed her love and approval. He needed to stay in her good graces. And he assumed that she needed him just as much.

He had a bad temper though. Sometimes he would get so angry that his emotions would erupt violently and overflow. The most foul words you could think of would rise up out of his throat and he could not control them. When he was fixed on getting his way, he chose to go beyond reason, into a highly volatile realm. And once the sequence had begun, he could not turn back midstream. He was committed to the full course until his anger saw an opportunity to relinquish its strength and die down. Sometimes, he became physically violent, throwing things and smashing things. So, it is no wonder that he went too far one day and killed his two brothers. They had threatened to expose the truth of him to their mother. He could not allow this loss of credibility to change his life.

But they continued to follow him for all of his long life. They were there, during the triumph of his days and during the nights when he wept as martyrs sometimes do. Oh, Fear and Ah, Bitterness were always there.

~~

Jacob abandoned his mother—whom he loved dearly— to escape punishment for his sins. And without even a goodbye, he ran away to the home of his uncle to be educated and raised.

At the local school, he became a proficient classicist, translating a Greek tragedy into Latin iambics by the age of fourteen. The next year, he began his study with some of the leading scholars of the time. And after having figured out the world, he found himself bored with the prevailing philosophy. He decided to redefine the world based upon his belief system and teach the way that it should be to the leaders and citizens. But he was young and few leaders were interested in his proposal and even fewer citizens had time to listen or take him seriously.

Upon his teacher's recommendation, at the age of twenty, he became a tutor to one of the most influential families in the area. This virtually lifelong association provided him with an extensive private library, foreign travel, and introductions to many important people.

Jacob was slow in developing his own ideas and they were not very original when they came to him. But, it was a natural gift for him to examine an existing belief, which appeared to be suspect, and critique the intent, judge its value and report his findings. Anyone who had time to listen could receive a lengthy report, sarcastically delivered, amusing. He was the expert in the world and his words were accepted as truth. He cut down the beliefs of others when they did not agree with his own. This method evolved to be his way. He was seldom challenged. In the war of words, he always won. He was the respected authority.

As a philosopher, his lectures were eloquent and he spoke with understanding on each political, social and scientific issue. He was well read and as he read, every word was examined as he critiqued the usage and context. And his standards were extremely high.

Jacob had a keen interest and high aptitude for mathematics. He spent dozens of hours thinking about and developing complex mathematical formulas. These were the basis for important inventions, discoveries and music, which very few could understand but at which all would marvel. In this, he was quite gifted.

With so many accomplishments under his belt, he became accustomed to the spotlight. He longed to travel and teach the world the knowledge he had acquired, and present his philosophy. And acting upon this longing, he made his way to the major cities, lecturing and teaching the young masters of the day. As a guest in their homes, he lived nominally, preferring to save the money he earned and to live off the trappings of the rich who retained him. Over time, he was able to build up a great amount of treasure.

It was during one such appointment that a visiting nobleman sought his advice in organizing the population in his prefecture. He wanted to create a model for peaceful coexistence among all of the people—a perfect society. Jacob wasted no time giving his view.

"Sir, peaceful coexistence is a matter of laws. If we tell the people how they must act, what is the proper dress and thought, then they will know and understand what is best for everyone. This is the chief purpose of education.

"Of course", said Jacob slyly, "your power over the citizens is absolute and should not be subject to the same laws and obligations. They will obey you as long as you fulfill the social agreement. Protect their right to earn a living. This is your obligation to them. This is the basis for peaceful coexistence in well-run societies.

"People shouldn't be allowed to do everything they can think of or desire. Think of the worst that can happen. There would be all manner of perversion around you", he said with a gnarled face. "People want to be controlled. They must be controlled and history has proven that motivating them to follow the moral code is the primary method of success. Having a good set of rules is vitally important!"

Jacob's passionate monologue convinced the nobleman that his model was for the best interest of all of the people. Everyone would benefit. And even though the nobleman did not fully understand the consequences of Jacob's plans, still, he was impressed by his display of confidence and knowledge. He put his trust in Jacob and all of his resources at Jacob's disposal.

"Come and work with me", urged the nobleman, "organizing the people while I am away and I will give you a high position drafting the laws of the land and teaching the people what is right and wrong." And Jacob graciously accepted.

~~

Now how could Jacob be sure of what was right and wrong for all people? It was clear that he needed rules to govern his own life so he wouldn't lie or kill or curse. He seemed to need boundaries so he would know when too far was TOO FAR. But could he assume that all people must be governed by the same rules? How would he know unless he consulted with those who were affected? Perhaps he believed that he was a god. Perish the thought.

Jacob's logic for the model society lay in the past—in actions and reactions, opinions of those who owned the land. He had dined, drank bitter wine and discussed the problem of laborers and the lack of moral laws with noblemen before. They had parted congratulating one other on their beliefs. And though he had never even spoken with those who break their backs to work the land, he felt confident that he knew what laws must be written.

~~

He wrote the laws eloquently, emphasizing the literal and clear interpretation in his writing. Many of his ideas were obvious suggestions but he wanted no misunderstanding. His words were to become symbols of remembrance, deeply significant and clear. He labored long on this. And when he had completed his task, he posted his well thought out creation, written on parchment, in the square.

The people flocked around the posting to read the news. Upon reading the new laws, one fourth of the people nodded in silence, agreeing that it must be this way for peace. One fourth of the people tore the parchment into tiny scraps and burned them, stomping them into the ground. They rebelled against cause, change. They shouted at Jacob. "These so called laws are not for progress. I don't think so! We won't do it!" One fourth of the people pondered the value of such laws and examined the evidence in support of and against such laws. One fourth of the people complained bitterly to Jacob, crying aloud, weeping.

"What have we done to offend you that you do this to us? These laws read like threats or ultimatums. Have we no choices? Have you no care in your heart for the suffering that will surely come from this? Don't you feel bad for what you are doing to us?"

After they wept, the fourth group became outraged.

"This is not the fair government that we asked for."

The third group continued to examine the truth of the laws among themselves and the long-term effect. They developed their conclusions. They contemplated the future but could not see how the laws would lead to peaceful coexistence, only trouble and a lifetime of conflict and persecution. But still they debated the issues.

Jacob spoke with the first of them and they continued to nod in support of him, smiling at him. He felt encouraged. He turned to the second group and tried to console them. But they would not hear him and turned their backs. He spoke to the third group but they were huddled in a great debate and did not nod yes or no. So, he took their silence for agreement. And with his confidence high, he turned to the fourth group commanding them to follow the laws or die! And there was silence throughout the square.

When he had finished chastising the fourth group, he calmed down and spoke rationally.

"All I ask", said Jacob, "is that you give this new method a chance before complaining. This is being done for the good of all. This is being done for you. Life will be better in this prefecture after we institute these laws."

But the dissenters continued to mumble and grumble, preparing themselves for war. The analyzers reviewed the facts along with documented outcomes of similar approaches from the past, considering the best approach.

Jacob saw that these, the dissenters and analyzers, were ungrateful after all of his hard work. He could not appreciate the differences between them, or the difference between his beliefs and theirs. He turned his back to their cries for alternatives, angrily throwing his papers to the ground. And with a smooth turn of his head, he stomped his way back to familiar territory seeking comfort.

~~

In the weeks that followed, one fourth of the citizens worked the land, complying with the new laws without complaint. A few citizens abandoned their jobs and left the valley for better opportunities. One fourth of them adhered to the laws while they secretly worked on a plan to change their condition. These sought the advice of a sage. Someone who could unify them and help them end the persecution without bloodshed. They found one in secret and from the beginning, she began to strategize, teaching them how to achieve freedom through humble long-suffering.

The fourth group plotted a rebellion. They sought a warrior, a leader who was willing to crush Jacob using his own tactics—a verbal war. They searched but could find no warrior willing to sacrifice himself. But a mediator heard their cries for help and went swiftly to meet with them.

~~

The rebellion had begun and now Jacob was forced to rally troops and enforce the laws he had written.

"What is this madness?" He wept alone. "I am doing everything I can for them. How could they not see that this is for the good of the whole? Without these laws, there would be chaos. Mankind must have the proper character, the appropriate look and the acceptable desires to live in harmony. If they just follow my instructions, we will all have peace!"

Jacob was impelled toward this mission. He was chosen for this task. It was molded into his plasma. And he had something to prove, to absolve himself of his past sins, to receive the blessing and the glory from his father and mother whom he had not seen for many years.

He was committed to this path. He could not turn back now for if he did he would lose his power and become a joke to be mocked.

"I am in charge here."

He insisted that everyone should know this and treat him with respect. Besides how much harm can a few peasants do when he had the law on his side? He was right, powerful and just.

~~

The problem, however, if you choose to call it a problem, is that Jacob was limited because of his short range of influence. Even now, in the midst of so much controversy, the idea that Jacob was the weak force did not occur to him. It never came up. He was the first and everyone in the world was measured by his standard, which was morally high. But this was of no consequence since he only partially adhered to his own standard.

~~

The fourth one was coming from the west to do battle with him—a mediator. He had never met her, but he had seen her in his dreams and turned his back to her, finding her light too bright. He had heard about her free spirit and some part of him secretly longed to know it. So, it is no wonder that he sat waiting anxiously for her arrival as he had been warned that she would come and he was well prepared.

The challenger had followed Jacob's career with interest all of her young life. She knew him well. She had questioned him before taking his knowledge as her own. She would question him again. And yet, she was mystical to him, unapproachable, untouchable like fog on a damp night. She was from a place moral people dare not look. For Jacob, it was an instinctively evil place, supernatural, a place to be feared.

He sat smugly waiting her arrival.

"Who is she to challenge me?" Jacob laughed.

~~

Before she ever arrived, there was a misunderstanding between them. The fourth simply wanted to understand Jacob's idealism. She had a strong penchant for rules herself. They smoothed out life and took away some of the guesswork. But still, she did not fully appreciate his methods. She had come to him to learn from him and once she understood his ideals, then she would convince him that he was wrong.

She wasted no time as she entered the city, but went straight to the point. Without making an arrangement to see him, she arrived on his doorstep and entered without knocking.

~~

The woman Seraph was known to be electric because of her high energy, which was contagious. She gave those she touched strength, the strength to bend, the power to expand their choices and even more, their lives.

She was a natural mediator with a selfless, empathetic connection to all types of beings—man, beast, birds, water creatures, even the earth itself. When charged up, she had a magnetic attraction to which a person was either drawn into her high sensitivity or repulsed by her conviction. To this end, she was loved or hated, followed or feared.

~~

Seraph was born last of the four, beautiful with black hair that stood straight up on her small round head as if it were electrically charged. Her pale yellow skin, which was nearly translucent, was smooth and fine. Perfectly aligned were her tiny features. And everyone who saw her said 'what a lovely child she is, so beautiful'. She was immediately proclaimed good by everyone who saw her.

One day, during the year that she was twelve, she went to the pasture where it was her task to feed the animals each day. And after ending her negotiations with them, she lay down in the tall grass and fell asleep. Her long black hair was a stark contrast against the golden wheat and she seemed to be floating above the ground. As she dreamed, she heard a voice speak to her.

"Follow the way!"

"What way", she asked, but there was no reply. She looked around and saw no one.

The next day, she took the same path to the pasture, fed the animals as she had been instructed, and afterward, lay down upon the grass looking into the sky. Presently, she fell asleep and dreamed. And in her dream, the heavens opened up, and she saw visions of a being she believed to be God. As she looked around, she could see the whole earth and she was connected to it. She was spread out over the surface and within all things. And she was the earth. Her blood flowed to the same rhythm as the sap of every living tree, and the low tide and the high waves, as the stars and all of the creatures and throughout the exhibition of the seasons. And she held her breath, amazed.

She heard a tiny suggestion of a message, like a single breeze stroking her cheek. Then she felt a strong, broad hand take hold of her and she listened… intently. When the instructions were complete, she looked into the sky straining to see the face of the One that spoke to her but she could not. She had heard His name and she wanted to call it aloud. But she could not remember it.

"Why do you speak to me?" She finally asked.

"Because you can hear me." His voice was kind.

"Do you speak to others?"

"I speak to the human spirit in all of mankind. Some cannot hear because they are afraid to know. Some that can hear ignore the signs and the warnings preferring to follow their own way. Some misinterpret the words and seek evil perversions instead of spiritual benefits."

"But how can I know the difference?" she asked.

"Listen and learn and you will come to know."

And Seraph awakened and stood up slowly.

An eagle flying far overhead caught her eye and she stopped to watch it as it circled past. It was a rare sight, a recognized symbol of courage and power. It was a message to her that would mark this day and her conversation with the face of true power.

She stood up and followed the eagle until she could see it no longer. Then she paced herself, stopping to smell the wild flowers and stroking the scale like leaves of a cypress tree before she thoughtfully headed home.

~~

She continued to dream these dreams. She followed the signs that were revealed to her and used them to prophesy to others. Telling them the future and advising them.

As she grew older, she found that she had a love of history and *all* things of beauty. The events of the past awakened her consciousness. She began to notice how close her own dreams were to the ancient myths and rituals practiced by the early tribes of man.

Seraph wanted to learn more. She read everything available to her, gobbling up every morsel. And when she had tapped out the available written resources, she set out on a quest to discuss her findings and compare her conclusions with *the open ones* who would listen.

At first, she could find no one. She was ignored and whispered about. They were afraid of her because *she spoke to spirits.* So, she moved on and became a chameleon. She adapted to fit into any group. She could become indistinguishable from the others. Then, as their trust in her increased, she began to question them, tapping into their knowledge, challenging their beliefs. Teaching them her way and insisting that it was right. Demanding that they should follow her ideals. Overtime, she grew to know everything and was convinced of this.

And yet, there were times when she felt as if she were mad and alone, even unreal. Certainly, she was misunderstood. She was the mystical center of an ongoing controversy. Her experience in this area attracted her to *victims.* Their causes gave her life purpose, glory. She was their saviour. Controversy was an outlet for her survival. Through it, she accepted her spiritual connection with the universe. This connection was a primary and inborn part of her humanness. Her life was but a dream.

~~

And so it was that Seraph's dreams led her to Jacob's assembly room late in the day, where he sat, writing letters, or warnings, documenting events and names, his philosophical ideals. She had come as the commissioned counselor campaigning against cruelty. She was the defense for free speech and civil liberties, rights of victims. The first round of conflict was about to begin.

~~

When she entered the room, Jacob raised his head and leaned back in his chair, relaxing his center in a posture of great authority. He raised one eyebrow and observed her—the enemy. She looked so different from him. She must be the demon they said she was. He had heard so much about her, rumors, gossip. What he had heard, he did not like. He expected her to attack him. She did not.

Seraph observed his actions, detecting his size and depth. She could see that they were both good people—intelligent, well traveled, quality. Only their missions were different.

She eased into the conversation by admiring his success, relating an experience or two, and listening to him proudly tell of his journeys and achievements. She was subtle, conforming to his way and feeding his ego to earn his trust.

Jacob, unfortunately, could not see the same goodness in her. His vision was clouded by his goal. Her values were not his. And he felt clearly superior.

~~

Now, the source of goodness, whatever the term may mean to the reader, comes from within oneself, it is not introduced from the outside. Jacob kept his goodness hidden, so that no one could take advantage of him. This was something he feared. He had learned through his experiences that goodness made you an easy target, vulnerable. Seraph extended her goodness outward to the family, to the community and to the victims, creatures and living things. She did this freely. In her experience, not only was goodness easy to acquire, but the more you give it away, the more glory you receive.

The theme of Jacob's battle was right or wrong, moral purpose, principle. Seraph had not come to battle. She had come seeking knowledge and understanding. She was fulfilling her spiritual purpose as a mediator for the oppressed. But too much of this talk will make one weak. Time was passing. The discussion was underway. The midnight hour had come and so far, nothing had been accomplished.

~~

"Jacob, why are you so fixed on your ideals that you cannot see the damage that you cause to others? I need to understand your way so we can come to an agreement."

Jacob was very willing to explain his position, as he believed strongly in the truth of it. It was his conviction. But what was this talk of agreement? There would be no agreement. He spoke calmly at first, but after a while, he grew weary of her questioning him and sought to shut her down.

"*Demon*, what are you talking about? Why are you asking me these questions? Why didn't you consult your spirits for the answers you seek? I have no enemies. I have seen no misery in this city and these laws are the laws these people asked for. My only role is to enforce them."

"Ah, Jacob. You are a liar! How stubborn and self-righteousness you are. You seem to be reasonable and intelligent. Why won't you listen to reason?"

"Listen to reason? Who are you that I should listen to you? Nobody. Now get out of my face."

Seraph raised an accusing finger and pointed it toward his heart.

"If you don't stop this now, Jacob, there will be war and devastation before there is peace. Hundreds will die needlessly."

Jacob smirked.

"The goal of every war is peace. So, let there be war if there must be peace. I am also a peaceful man."

"And at what cost? You carry balance scales in your sack of tools and tricks, but you do everything you can to ensure that they tip in your favor. You have a fire in your heart, which strengthens your resolve to do evil. It seeks out and destroys the lives of those you fear. How many must die broken-hearted and lost for your bit of peace, Jacob? Tell me that!"

"Who do you think you are?" Jacob spoke in a low and chilling tone. His tongue became sharp like a double-edged sword…and poisonous. He threatened her within an inch of her life and she was powerless to strike back. He called her vile names and shouted insults, which struck her hard in the face. The weak force controlled his tongue. He grabbed her accusing hand and began to bend it back as if he would break it, watching her face for signs of pain, which came quickly. The strong force controlled his hands. He spewed out the venom of his heart—angry, bitter and reproachful. She tried to get away but he was holding her arm tightly and she could not move.

He began to question her, demanding an answer in their absurd ballet.

"Who sent you here?" asked Jacob.

"No one. I saw the suffering and came to reason with you. Please let me go!"

"Who sent you here?" asked Jacob.

"I came on my own. Now please let me go!"

"Who sent you here?" asked Jacob speaking slowly and more agitated, bullying her and taking pleasure in it.

And she gave him the same reply but in a new way, with different words. But he was relentless. He did not back down. He did not cower under her stare. His grimace threatened to become more dangerous and he was still holding her arm tightly.

The course that was programmed was clear—on automatic pilot. He was spinning into a rage, uncontrollable. If this ballet were to be stopped before the final act, she would have to stop it. She softened and looked into his face, gravely serious and spoke slow.

"I can tell that you have suffered a great deal, Jacob, making the decisions you have made and trying to continue to uphold them. You have shown that you have what it takes to be a great leader."

Jacob opened his eyes wide and turned his head to look her full in the face. He immediately lowered his defenses and accepted this judgment knowing that she spoke the truth of him. He agreed with her and began to explain his position more clearly, giving her the background and the pieces she lacked. His ego was being fed by her praise. And he clearly wanted more of the same. And he clearly wanted more of the same.

Seraph ceased to struggle against him and he let her go. She allowed him to talk and she listened while Jacob's own words condemned his ways. He told her about his life, his triumphs and disappointments. She heard the story of his brothers and of their deaths and of his piteous life since and she wept sorrowfully for him and held his hand in compassion. She understood now that this fight would be better fought in the courts. He would not change. He had only one full view of reality and he resolutely followed it. His choices were limited. And what a difficult past he had had. Full of sadness and suffering. She empathized with him and pitied him. In one swift turn, she surrendered to him and vowed her allegiance to protect him and do all that she could to help him achieve his goal. He deserved her support for he had suffered the greatest. And this was true.

She smiled at him, understanding this, though in her heart she did not fully agree. Life for him was black or white, right or wrong. Who was she to say it should be otherwise?

Just before daylight, she wiped her tears and his and turned to leave and he lunged forward and grabbed her arm and pulled her back. She looked into his eyes and they were full of sadness.

"Bless me, right now, before you go", he whispered.

She looked into his eyes and saw the smoldering embers from the fire of the weak force as it died down and out. Then she prayed for God's mercy on him and after he had heard the words, he stared at her long and hard. Then he asked.

"Who are you, really?"

"I am Seraph, your sister. I thought you knew me."

He loosened his hold on her and stepped back. He closed his eyes to erase the thoughts he had in his heart. And Jacob became quiet, contemplating life's cruel jokes.

When she had departed and the soft thud of the door hit the frame, he ran to the door and looked to see what direction she had gone but he could not see her. Seraph disappeared into the misty dawn. And he blinked his eyes and wondered if this angel had been there at all.

~~

The father had arrived like a thief and witnessed his children in battle. And when it was over, he followed Jacob in secret the short distance to his doorstep. He stood outside watching and heard the closing of the door, the bolting of the locks, and saw the curtains being drawn tightly as his son, hid his collection of things and mounting indiscretions from the world. The father was overcome with sadness, and covered his face and wept. Only one of the four could physically stop Jacob. It was the warrior, Grace.

~~

And so, it is as it has always been. Man, a physical being, finds himself in conflict with the spirit, which he cannot see or understand. Man fights with one woman and wins and defines all women by this one, as weaker and less intelligent than he. And though he has seen only one fourth of the picture through her, he teaches the world, and the world accepts this view as a fact. But as usual, he has misunderstood her purpose and assigned his own two-dimensional values to a much larger picture.

~~

Then Jacob fearing pain and worse, annihilation, awakened after a testy nap and ran to another sister for advice and protection. And his father followed close behind.

~~

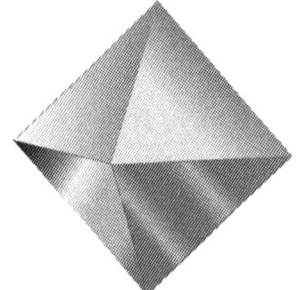 Grace, the second child, was born a great warrior. She came from the south and was the strong force, the strongest force even. She arrived through her mother's wound with sword in hand, slashing flesh and cutting down arteries to make her way into the world. And she was fearless and beautiful with spicy red cheeks and long auburn hair that grew down to her waist. Her eyes were wide with wonder from the very first moment and she was curious about everything she touched, heard, saw, felt and tasted.

From the day of her birth, Grace was in constant motion. The motion of her movements set the pace for those in her circle. They coordinated their movements to match the heat and energy, which was scattered about her. She had a commanding presence and she was difficult to resist.

All in all, she was good. Everyone who attended her birth believed it and proclaimed it so.

As a child, when she required special attention, she would pout, until she was rewarded with a special treat. If this method did not work, she would rise up out of herself, growing angry and stamp her feet, or bang the walls loudly to signal anyone who could hear and come to her aid. When she got older, she followed her passions in much the same way. If she really wanted it, she would not be denied. She would be seen and if not seen, heard or felt. In her youth, unlike Jacob, she acted upon her impulsive nature. Like Seraph, she often took her actions further, risked much more and sought a much higher level of satisfaction.

As a warrior, she was best known for holding the troops together through her high energy, direct words, radical moves and thoroughly unexpected compassion. With this combination, she accomplished much more than her fellow soldiers did in less than half the time.

As she quickly moved up the ranks, she used her contacts to gain access and to lead several key strategic initiatives, which were successful. For each of these, she brought home the rewards available to the victorious—the spoils.

Now all military operations are laden with level upon level of hierarchy. And with each win, the credit for the success went to the highest-ranking officer. This disturbed Grace a great deal since much of her natural motivation came from displaying her power, winning and the awe of her troops. She desired the top post; the highest tribute and credit for all of her hard won battles.

In a cunning moment, she planned for a secret meeting with members of the military council who had authority over her future. She used her beauty and natural curiosity to her advantage and was awarded the high post she sought.

Once she achieved this post, she found herself surrounded by enemies. Her direct words, her impulsiveness, and impatience had raised an eyebrow or two in the past, but this great big promotion left many of her subordinates gasping for air and clutching their chests. The enemy went to work immediately, making all sorts of accusations against her including unethical misconduct, and worse. Even the very troops she taught and gave her energy to and cared for now turned their backs on her considering her to be a traitor.

Over the next several months, she was surrounded by controversy. She looked around and saw those who were her juniors being promoted to a higher rank than hers. She became angry at the system. And she became disillusioned with the world and decided to run away. She submitted a letter of resignation. But a supporter in high places intervened and pleaded with her to stay and fight and wait for her reward that would surely come. And so, she stayed on.

In the spring, she had an opportunity for revenge on those who had turned against her and she jumped eagerly at the chance. She had learned through her spies of an attack, which would destroy the ammunition site just outside of her jurisdiction. She swiftly rounded up the militia and raced to meet the enemy. The skirmish was successful and a grateful council advanced her to Major General in command of Jacob's enforcement troops.

This title gave her a license to move in the aristocratic circles. Here the beautiful and bold Grace lived lavishly, far beyond her means. She soon found herself heavily in debt, resorting to schemes to maintain a lofty pretense for the public eye.

At the same time, she found herself being charged again with a number of offenses connected with using her high position for private gain. This time she was outraged by the charges. She thought she had risen above such suspicions. She was a Major General! Who charges the *leader* with a crime? The strong force rose up in her brain disconnecting her facility for reasoning from her physical actions. She shouted with all of her might, venting her frustrations to anyone who would listen—speaking quickly, throwing and grabbing, attacking the weak ones in her way.

"Who charges me? Come forward if you have the guts. Show me your motive, you worms. When I find you and I will, you will regret the day of your birth. This is my solemn promise. You will look for death, beg for it, but it won't come quickly enough for you to escape your suffering."

At night, all alone, she fought in her sleep and dreamed of getting even. She was broken by the betrayal of her men and she was sorely in need of money.

The next morning, she was up early, rearranging the furniture and dusting, sweeping the floor, trying to work off the anxious energy, which had built up during the night. It was in this state that Jacob found her when he arrived.

She heard the knock on the door and ignored it the first time. She heard the knock on the door and ignored it the second time. When the knock came the third time, she responded with an irritated scowl.

"What do you want?", she screamed.

"It's Jacob. May I come in?"

She marched to the door, and turned the knob cruelly. As the force of gravity relinquished its hold, the door flew back against her.

~~

"Jacob, what are you doing here? What do you want?" Grace said when she saw him.

"I came for a visit. It has been a while since we talked. I wanted to see how you were doing. I heard that you had some troubles. I can't tell. You look wonderful."

"Jacob, what do you want?" she yelled loudly, throwing her head back.

Jacob cleared his throat and swallowed hard touching his neck.

"I came to seek your advice on an issue that is very important. May I come in?"

She stared at him for a moment or two, contemplating this. Then she turned her back and continued her busywork.

"Make it quick. I have too much to do today to waste my time with you."

"Yes, yes. I will be quick."

He cleared his throat again and sat down before he began to speak and she continued to work.

"So many things are not going well for me, Grace. I do have troubles. Seraph came to me last night. I think she represents the rebels though I could not get her to admit it. Before she left though, she pledged allegiance to me. But how can I trust her? I need your advice on how to handle this whole rebellion. What should I do?"

Grace did not stop for one moment. She answered unconcerned.

"You put yourself in this position. You did not ask me for advice before you began. Don't ask my advice now. I am sure you will figure it out. Anything else?"

Jacob withered under her harsh rejection and felt as if he would faint. And seeing the uselessness of his life began to wail loudly, lamenting his condition.

"Why didn't I die at birth as I came from the womb? Why did my mother let me live? Why did she nurse me at her breasts? If I had died at birth, I would be at peace now, asleep and at rest. I would rest with the world's kings and prime ministers, famous and great. I would rest with wealthy princes whose palaces were filled with gold and silver. Why was I not buried like a stillborn child, like a baby who never lives to see the light or buried with my two brothers? For in death, the wicked cease from troubling, and the weary are at rest. Even prisoners are at ease in death, with no guards to curse them.

"Oh, why should light be given to the weary, and life to those in misery? Why is life given to those with no future, those destined by God to live in distress so they go around making the lives of good people miserable? And for what purpose? I cannot eat for sighing; my groans pour out like water. And don't I have a right to complain? Even babies cry when they are hungry. People complain when there is no salt in their food. And how tasteless is the uncooked white of an egg! My appetite disappears when I look at it; I gag at the thought of eating it! And yet, I am under attack, because I wrote the law. I did only what I was asked. I am blameless.

"What I always feared has happened to me. What I dreaded has come to be. I have no peace, no quietness. I have no rest; instead, only trouble comes. I live in fear now. I have no hope. Only bitter days lie ahead of me."

He sobbed. Then Grace who had begun to pace back and forth turned sharply to him, her face lit with contempt at the sound of his self-pity. She grabbed his forehead and shoved it back from his hands and spoke sternly to Jacob as he continued to sob.

"Stop your weeping and sit up. You are a fraud! I despise weakness and there is a great deal of weakness in you. Now stop whining and get out. I will not help you."

The strong force rose up as she grabbed his collar and threw him against the door. Kicking him angrily before she stomped out of the room.

Jacob rose up slowly and wiped his face. He loved Grace, but she had no love for him—not today. He could see the goodness in her for she was truly strong and he needed her strength. With his head hung down, he headed home.

When he had gone, she began to curse and scream loudly, knocking over the prized possessions that were in her way. She was dizzy from the power she exerted—the strong force. Her head and heart would explode. She unconsciously bit her tongue. She was reeling from this concentrated flow of energy that rose up out of her heart, uncontrolled.

Toward the end of her rampage, she sat down on a chair where she could gather herself and keep from losing consciousness. The energy dissipated and scattered, and she calmed down. She was overcome by a weaker force, an electromagnetic surge of emotion and she sobbed, softly.

"How long will you try to break me? Why must everyone watch me and demand an accounting from me? What am I supposed to do when God tempts me?"

She thought and thought, trying to know why. She conceded that this is life.

"How frail we are! Life is so short and full of trouble!"

In a while, she gathered herself back into an intelligent box, shrugged off her self-pity and donning her armour and her sword, she set out to consult with Solon. She needed the advice of a sage before she could proceed.

~~

The children were in battle—all but one so far. And the father seeing the shallowness of his children's lives knew that he had but a single hope to unify them. He must return to them and teach them the truth.

~~

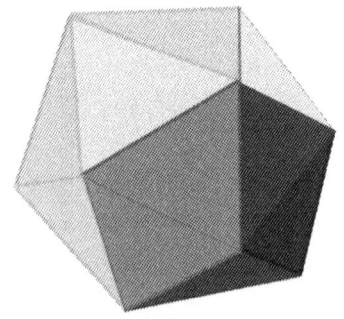

The sage Solon came out of the north. She was wise, indeed. But it was a little known fact since she cared so little for social formalities and seldom struck up a conversation with anyone. She only spoke when she knew it was required or if she was approached by others. The rest of the time, she held her tongue, preferring to observe, listen and learn.

It is true that she was considered strange, slow. But she was misunderstood. It was as if she was speaking in tongues, stuttering. The general population could not understand her. She did not fit the normal mold. She was socially inept and she kept to herself, out of the spotlight, in the shadows. While she hid, she concentrated on increasing her skills on the subjects she valued—linguistics, acrobatics, electronics, technology and mechanics—areas that require a high degree of precision. She needed to know why things worked—not just how. She learned slowly, experiencing each nuance. Then, she mastered the task and quickly moved on to learn something new, applying the principles she learned from the old.

Over time, the length of the learning cycle lessened and she would know the answer without analyzing the possibilities.

During her working years, she labored hard, long hours and without complaint about pay or working relationships. She knew her reward would come soon enough.

Her lifestyle was not of the normal type. She lived in utter seclusion unlike her brother Jacob and two sisters Grace and Seraph. These three needed each other for the fulfillment of their life purposes and daily assignments.

She did not take the wide road. She traveled the unfamiliar back roads, unnoticed. She did not follow the main stream of logic. She could not. Her dreams took her out way past common understanding and imagination. She found it difficult to communicate her passions to them. Jacob would hear her and cite the common conclusion or suggest an obvious remedy. Grace would listen but could seldom offer anything new. Even Seraph could not relate to Solon's ideals without a great many qualifications, clarifiers and time. Time was needed between conversations to absorb meaning and gain understanding. So, Solon spoke in syllogistic arguments and metaphors to make her meaning clear.

The three others were puzzled by her odd nature. They came to ignore her when she was present and made clever jokes about her in her absence. She was aware, though she seemed not to be. She did not defend herself with words. She did not defend herself at all. She held her tongue and waited, observing their ways. Then she explained their weaknesses to those who asked—pointing out their shortcomings and errors. She was not concerned with retaliation. She spoke the truth. And she knew that a time would come when they would seek her help and she would know the answers they sought.

~~

When Solon was born, the third child, she slipped quietly from the wound. Adjusting her pale eyes to the light, she could see the ceiling and the light that hung there clearly, but everything close to her was indistinguishable including her mother's face, whose arms held her close. Her skin was stark white as if she bore no blood, no heart and later it would come to be true...to those who had heard *about* her. But not true, to those who knew her. She did not cry and they thought she was deaf but she could hear very well. The visitors at her birth smiled sadly at her and pitied her, proclaiming that surely she was good.

For the first twelve years she did not speak. She was listening very closely and storing up everything she learned, blending and assimilating and drawing conclusions and looking for the truth. When she did begin to speak, she conformed to those around her imitating their words and way so that they would be comfortable with her strange ways. When she made a mistake, she was quick to apologize for her ignorance since words were not to be used for malice only good. But still she was misunderstood.

People gravitated to her slowly. She was always calm, too calm, suspiciously calm and her voice was even and low. Those who came to her found her silent and thoughtful, watching too closely. Three-quarters of the world was unfulfilled by her relentless silence and judged her to be incompetent. They could not understand her. But silence is like snow. It covers up a multitude of imperfections. And, unless you are perched very high in the mountains, eventually, even the loveliest of snow melts exposing the beauty of spring. She knew that the time would come when one would recognize her wisdom and be moved to tell the others. The truth of the prophecy was about to be fulfilled.

~~

Solon appeared to be somewhat simple, from the outside. But the dimensions of her mind were extremely complex. She had a natural connection with God. Through Him, she could see visions of the future. With her discernment and constant search for truth, she could unify diametrically opposed forces.

She began to develop non-violent strategies to overcome Jacob's moral persecution of the innocent in the world from the beginning. Teaching the people to persevere and wait. Yet, she knew too well, that there is a high degree of pointlessness in a non-violent war. The heart of the oppressor has to be moved before a change can come for the people oppressed. This would take time and maybe even stronger tactics and sacrifices. And she was prepared for this. When the persecuted came to her, she taught them to follow their intuition, to reach the intellectual conclusion, to search for the truth. Instinctual drives only increase the devastation in a war and many innocent are killed while the culpable are free to wander off.

~~

And so, it seemed that the whole world was at war. It was the season of death and destruction, chaos. Everyone, at every moment was attacking or retreating from an attack. From the outside it looked like it was a war of color, of gender, religion, nation against nation, mother and daughter, terrorist against capitalist, all within the human family. What a shame!

Jacob unknowingly incited chaos by imposing his values. Grace, annoyed by the disruption, ignored it in pursuit of her own desires. Solon could see and understand it and she taught the followers who came to her the truth of it. Seraph led the fight and supported Jacob, whom she loved. She believed that he would be the victor. She was fully convinced of this and loyal.

~~

In a war, there sometimes comes a moment when words are meaningless. The graveness of suffering takes an unbearable turn. The villians cannot see the truth of their actions. It is during these times that a message must be sent that the whole world can hear. It comes on the wings of a shrill sound that dulls the senses and speeds the heartbeat.

~~

But not today. Solon urged the people to resist violence and hold on for the change that was sure to come.

~~

Grace arrived late in the evening to explain her case and ask for Solon's support. And when she came into the house, she saw that it was bare except for a well-made bed and a chair, which Solon offered to Grace. The room was stark white and naked except for an oddly shaped crystal, which hung from the ceiling low, almost midway to the floor. It was a complex looking structure with twelve solid walls of clear glass, each bound by five equilateral plane triangles, and twenty faces. Grace stepped around it, barely noticing it, passing the chair to move closer to Solon but Solon stopped her.

"Grace, stay where you are so that I may see you clearly."

Grace stood near the structure, bowing her head to see past the glare of the light and waited for Solon's acknowledgment. After some time, she sat down in the chair.

Solon, sat on the floor next to a teakettle and holding a cup to her lips, she took a sip and it was bitter. They sat together in this fashion for several minutes until Grace, who could contain herself no longer, took a deep breath and began to speak.

"Solon, my experience shows that those who plant trouble and cultivate evil will harvest the same. I accept that and know that we, who are fierce young lions, will all be broken and destroyed eventually. No one wants us to succeed. They want us to scatter, to break us down so that we will starve and beg them for food to feed our young. That's why I live for today. I will never beg. I take what I want from the earth. I am powered by it. It is my way.

"The other night, I dreamed and a vision came to me as others slept. Fear gripped me; I trembled and shook with terror. A spirit swept past my face. Its wind sent shivers up my spine. It stopped, but I couldn't see its shape. There was a form before my eyes, and a hushed voice said, 'Can a mortal be just and upright before God? Can a person be pure before the Creator?' And I have thought long and hard about this every night afterward.

"I don't know all of the answers to life's mysteries, but this I do know. If God cannot trust His own angels and has charged some of them with folly, how much less will He trust us who are made of clay? Our foundation is dust, Solon, and we are crushed as easily as moths that are alive in the morning, but by evening, they are dead, gone forever without a trace. Their hearts collapse and they die in ignorance never knowing why they existed at all. That's why I live zealously, each moment. Capturing as much of life as I can. In my experience, a fool may be successful for a moment, but then comes the sudden disaster that leaves us yearning for pity."

Grace sat back and contemplated for a moment on her own words. And while she thought, Solon was thoughtful. It was a simple matter for her to see the depth of Grace's wisdom. But she was somehow uncomfortable with Grace understanding so much and shifted her weight under the glare of this honesty, this candor. She had expected the same foolish, materialistic child that she once knew. In the meanwhile, Grace continued.

"If my sadness could be weighed and my troubles be put on the scales, they would be heavier than all the sands of the sea. For all the good I have done, I have no one and nothing. I know I have behaved rashly. I was given a task and I was overjoyed for it. I set about it with all of my heart, in good faith, pouring out my heart to win and make my superiors proud. I did not begin this journey with evil intentions. Then my men mocked my name and set themselves against me. I felt as if the Almighty had struck me down with His arrows. As if He had sent His poisoned arrows deep within my spirit and His terrors were arrayed against me.

"Solon, I do not have the strength to endure this trial. I do not have a goal that encourages me to carry on. Do I have strength as hard as stone? Is my body made of bronze? No, I am utterly helpless, without any chance of success. Solon, I need your guidance. What should I do?"

Solon looked at Grace's face and it was contorted with suffering. But Solon knew that if she got involved now that the consequences would come back to haunt her. She had too much at stake to take such a chance. Hundreds were counting on her to help them defeat Jacob's laws. An affiliation with Grace, Jacob's general, would send a signal that Solon had betrayed her charges. She thought about what she may be able to do to help but she had no silver bullet, no solution. She had not been consulted before Grace began in her wayward direction. How could she be expected to stand beside her now? Weighing the future of the whole prefecture against Grace's future, the choice was clear. She could not stand behind Grace. The decision was made.

"Grace, I have thought about your situation. As you say, you are in a grave spot. Your lack of funds will hurt you and you could be facing imprisonment. So you have two options. This may be a time for you to get away. Begin again. On the other hand, you have learned a great deal. I can tell that you are much wiser than your foolish beginnings. But there is still a great deal that you don't know. Face your accusers and repent your wrongdoing and learn your lessons. I will place your name before those who can help you. And after your punishment is spent, we can discuss the future."

"I can't run away. What will they think of me? I have no money! I thought you would be more sympathetic."

"Grace, you have followed your senses into this day. No one has done this to you. You have done it to yourself. If you want, I can give you money enough to get away, but you will have to face your accusers some time. Isn't today as good a day as any?"

"Yes, maybe. But I thought that you would help me, give me some good advice that I could use. And, maybe make a potion to help me ward off the evil that is coming to me."

Solon laughed.

"I have no magic tricks! No tarot cards. No superhuman strength. No disappearing acts. I don't read minds. I have no talisman other than my good name, my influence. I cannot turn water into wine or evil hearts into good. I am an ordinary woman just as your are."

They both sat staring at each other for a time. Then Grace broke the silence.

"Will you bless me then?"

"I will pray for you and God will bless you."

When she lifted up her eyes, the door flew open. Seraph strode in swiftly with her weapon drawn, convinced, knowing everything and fully ready for a battle. She ran straight into the prism, which was hanging low in the center of the room. When she had recovered, she wasted no time before she attacked, her finger pointing at Solon's heart. She looked into Seraph's face and saw that she was not herself. A force had taken her mind and heart over. Her face was distorted, terrifying, frightening and very powerful. Her teeth seemed to be made of iron, large with the power to crush and devour anyone in the way. The spirit in her heart was angry enough to murder and then trample underfoot whatever may be left of the prey. She was clearly different from the other three.Seraph let out a sound that began low like the rumbling of thunder. In one swift movement, she drew her sword and bending backward, she gathered her power to strike.

"Solon, you have been accused of committing treason against the state. I know that you have helped the rebels organize and prepared them for battle. You will be hanged in less than a fortnight. Prepare yourself for judgment day, for you will surely die!"

Jacob walked into the room slowly, stepping around the oddly shaped prism hanging in the center of the room. He had managed to accomplish his purpose without lifting a finger and looked smugly at Solon who never uttered a word. Grace stood up and challenged Seraph's accusation.

"Where is your proof?"

"I talked to several people who said that they overheard her talking to the analyzers and rebels. I was told that they had joined forces against Jacob and were preparing to march against him. Jacob has only done what he was asked to do. He is blameless. What right has Solon to crush his dreams? Besides, I suspected something was going on in here. She is too quiet. Too much silence means something is hidden. She never talks to me. She just stares. People have died for this cause and she had never even shed a tear. She has shown no remorse. Her heart is cold and evil, if she has a heart at all."

~~

The trial had begun. But no sooner had it started than the case collapsed flat, if there was ever any case at all. Jacob, Grace and Seraph argued among themselves, neither gaining ground over the other, just yelling foul, cutting each other off and insulting one another. And Solon sat alone.

Jacob could not hear himself think. He wanted Solon's support and he was willing to listen to her wise words. He broke away from the threesome while Grace and Seraph competed ruthlessly against each other for a prize that neither of them could ever claim.

"Solon", said Jacob sitting on the floor close beside her. "I know you are on trial, but I need your help. I really don't know what has happened."

"How can I help you, Jacob?"

He was surprised at her agreeableness, her tender voice. He expected her to be angry, but she smiled at him and reached out her hand to him.

"In my past, I would never have refused to help the poor, or crushed the hopes of those who looked to me for help. Whenever I saw someone who was homeless and without clothes, did they not praise me for providing clothing to keep them warm? And now what hope do I have to help them if they do not follow the law?"

Solon was tired. She looked at the floor for strength. She needed a firm foundation to help her through this.

"Jacob, Are you ready for the truth or do you want to hear shallow words to ease your guilt?"

"Well, I… am ready for the truth. I have no other options."

"Then stop passing it by."

"What do you mean?" asked Jacob.

"You have passed the truth by many times seeking the answers you want to hear, vanity, full of smoke. Like the prism hanging from the ceiling, truth is an annoyance to you, hanging so low and yet you ignore it. And after you pass by it twice, you brush it out of the way. And after you pass it three times, you can no longer see it. You have the truth, Jacob. Search yourself."

"I knew that you wouldn't help me. You are nothing. You will get exactly what you deserve. I condemn you."

"Jacob, it is better for you to find the truth and know that it is, than for me to tell you. What is the good in that? If I give you my way, it will only confuse you. And you will blame me when it does not end well. How can I advise you?"

"You are harsh in your judgment of me. But I guess I knew you would be."

"Jacob, you have put your trust in knowledge and felt secure because of your gold. Your happiness has depended on your wealth and that which you own. You have looked at the sun shining in the skies, or the moon walking down its silver pathway, and been secretly enticed in your heart to worship them. You have denied your father. You have killed your brothers. You have rejoiced when your enemies came to ruin and became excited when harm came their way. You have cursed your enemies and prayed for revenge. The people have gone hungry on your account and in your fear, you have turned away strangers seeking direction or a place to sleep.

"You have tried to hide these sins as men normally do, locking your guilt in a closet. But now you fear the crowd and their contempt. You have refused to acknowledge your errors to the public you have harmed. And as a condition of your mistake, you cannot go outside. You are a prisoner, just as I am. Locked away without love or safety.

"I know all of this!" shouted Jacob. "You don't have to tell me. These things I do know. If only I had someone who would listen to me and try to see my side! I know that I was right to create the laws in this way. I can see no other possibilities. Can you show me that I am wrong? Let the accuser write out my crimes if he dares to do it!"

Solon, knowing the history spoke quietly to Jacob, calming him and bringing his energy down to a rational level so that she could help him to think.

"Jacob, what method did you use to determine what laws should be included and which should not? Did you ask the people who would have their freedom taken away what they required?"

"My client is the nobleman. He is the one who pays me. We spoke and he gave me his requirements. That is all. I swear to you by all that is right that I have done nothing wrong."

"Surely your nobleman is not an evil man. Surely his intent was to ensure happiness and safety, even peace for the whole society."

"Yes, but I planned this to be a model society governed with these brilliant laws. Everyone would look upon it and say great things about the citizens and life would be perfect. My father and mother would accept me again."

"Perfect for whom?"

Jacob would not answer. He sat shaking his head. And yet, he knew the answer. He looked into a far off place and saw the whole picture unfold slowly, understanding his error.

And then, the father, old, tired and gray with disappointment decided it was time to come again.

~~

When they heard him enter, they felt his presence and stopped their idle chatter midstream. They all looked at him wide-eyed with fear and guilt on their faces, trying to determine the reason for his visit. Then he began to speak, honoring them, chastising them, pointing out the consequences of their ways and the remedies to save their souls. And they knew it was judgment day and they were all afraid.

~~

"Jacob, you are a man among three intelligent women. You are a solid foundation—a great philosopher, a man of many words, with great knowledge. You have the facts and a high aptitude for mathematics and music. You have an important mission to teach all that you know to any who will hear it.

"I know that you are surrounded by evil, and yet you have remained loyal to me. And you refused to deny me even when my faithful witness was martyred by Satan's followers.

"And yet, I have a few complaints against you. You have a pair of scales in your hand and these have been used to advance your purposes, not mine. Justice should be tempered with mercy. You are the one who has a sharp two-edged sword—it is your words. Words should be used to build up, not to tear down. Words should be used for truth, not for lies."

The father's words shocked Jacob and there was silence throughout the room for about half an hour. Then he continued.

"Jacob, these are you choices: You must be quick to listen, slow to speak, and slow to get angry. Your anger can never make things right. Get rid of all the filth and evil in your life, and humbly accept the message I have planted in your heart, for it is strong enough to save your soul. And remember, it is a message to obey, not just to listen to. If you don't obey, you are only fooling yourself. If you just listen and don't obey, it is like looking at your face in a mirror but doing nothing to improve your appearance. You see yourself, walk away, and forget what you look like. But if you keep looking steadily at my perfect law—the law that sets you free—and if you do what it says and don't forget what you heard, then I will bless you for doing it.

"And Jacob, If you claim to be religious but don't control your tongue, you are just fooling yourself, and your religion is worthless. Pure and lasting religion means that you must also care for orphans and widows in their troubles, and refuse to let the world corrupt you or entice you.

"If you are wise and understand my ways as you claim, live a life of steady goodness so that only good deeds will pour forth. And if you don't brag about the good you do, then you will be truly wise! But if you are bitterly jealous and there is selfish ambition in your heart, don't brag about being wise. That is the worst kind of lie. For jealousy and selfishness is not my kind of wisdom. Such things are earthly, unspiritual. For wherever there is jealousy and selfish ambition, there you will find disorder and every kind of evil. But wisdom is first of all pure. It is also peace loving, gentle at all times, and willing to yield to others. It is full of mercy and good deeds. It shows no partiality and is always sincere. And those who are peacemakers will plant seeds of peace and reap a harvest of goodness.

"But most of all, my son, never take an oath, by heaven or earth or anything else. Just say a simple yes or no, so that you will not sin and be condemned for it.

"If you are suffering, you should pray and keep on praying about it. And if you have reason to be thankful, continually sing praises. If you are sick, then call for the elders of the church and have them pray over you. Prayers offered in faith will heal. And if you have committed sins, they will be forgiven. Confess your sins to each other and pray for each other so that you may be healed. The earnest prayer of a righteous person has great power and wonderful results.

"My dear son, if anyone wanders away from the truth and is brought back again, you can be sure that the one who brings that person back will save that sinner from death and bring about the forgiveness of many sins.

"Now Jacob, if you fail to follow these instructions you can expect these consequences. Toward the end of your days, a great flaming star will fall out of the sky, burning like a torch. And the name of the star will be Bitterness. It will touch everything in your life and it will be bitter. And you and your descendents will die because your lives are so full of resentment and wrathful indignation.

"But if you give thanks to the one who is and who always was and put away your pride and anger, you will receive a great reward. Repent Jacob, or I will come to you suddenly and fight against you with the sword of my mouth and your words will have no meaning.

"And last, I advise you to buy gold from me—gold that has been purified by fire. Then you will be rich. And also buy white garments so you will not be shamed by your nakedness. Buy ointment for your eyes so you will be able to see. Be diligent and turn from your indifference.

"Look Jacob! Here I stand at your door and knock. If you hear me and open the door, I will come in. And we will share a meal as friends. And I will invite you to sit with me on my throne."

And Grace, Solon and Seraph formed a circle around Jacob to show their compassion, and comfort him, and show empathy for him. The blood in their hearts was pounding hard and their nostrils were wide open. And with their eyes opened wide and staring forward, they looked as if they were frozen together like one man instead of four. Then Jacob fell on his knees and wept. The father turned to Grace and began to speak again.

~~

"High spirited Grace, you are truly a great warrior. The lion, the first to arrive and the last to leave. You have been at the very brink of death many times and yet you are alive. I know you and you are holy and true. You have the key, which opens doors that no one can shut, and that closes doors that no one can open. With eyes like flames of fire, you and your mighty sword have the authority and power to remove peace from the face of the earth. But then...there would be war and slaughter everywhere and who would be able to survive it?

"Grace, I know about your suffering and your poverty—but you are rich! I know the slander of those opposing you. Don't be afraid of what you are suffering. Remain faithful, even when facing death and I will give you a crown of life.

"I know all of the things you do and I have opened a door for you that no one can shut. You have little strength to resist temptation, and yet you obeyed my word and did not deny me. Look! I will force those who are liars to come and bow down at your feet. They will acknowledge that you are the one I love. Because you have obeyed my command to persevere, I will protect you from the great time of testing.

"But Grace, I have a few issues to bring to your attention. First, remember that no one who wants to do wrong should ever say, 'God is tempting me.' God is never tempted to do wrong, and He never tempts anyone else either. Temptation comes from the lure of your own evil desires. These evil desires lead to evil actions, and evil actions lead to death. So don't be misled, my child. Whatever is good and perfect comes to you from God. He never changes or casts shifting shadows. In His goodness, He has given you His true word. And humankind, out of all creation, became His choice possession.

"Grace, we all make many mistakes, but those who control their tongues can also control themselves in every other way. You can make a large horse turn around and go wherever you want by means of a small bit in its mouth. And a tiny rudder makes a huge ship turn wherever the pilot wants it to go, even though the winds are strong. So also, the tongue is a small thing, but what enormous damage it can do. A tiny spark can set a great forest on fire. And the tongue is a flame of fire. It is full of wickedness that can ruin your whole life. It can turn the entire course of your life into a blazing flame of destruction, for it is set on fire by hell itself. People can tame all kinds of animals and birds and reptiles and fish, but no one can tame the tongue. It is an uncontrollable evil, full of deadly poison. Sometimes it sings praises to God, and sometimes it breaks out into curses against those who have been made in the image of God. And so, blessing and cursing come pouring out of the same mouth. Surely, this is not right! Does a spring of water bubble out with both fresh water and bitter water? Can you pick olives from a fig tree or figs from a grapevine? No, and you can't draw fresh water from a salty pool.

"Look here, you rich woman, weep and groan with anguish because of all the terrible troubles ahead of you. Your wealth is rotting away, and your fine clothes are moth-eaten rags. Your gold and silver have become worthless. The very wealth you were counting on will eat away your flesh. The treasure you have accumulated stands as evidence against you today. For listen! Hear the cries of the field workers whom you have cheated of their pay. The wages you held back cry out against you. The cries of the reapers have even reached my ears. You have spent your years on earth in luxury, satisfying your every whim. Now your heart is nice and fat, ready for the slaughter. You have condemned and killed good people who had no power to defend themselves against you.

"Now Grace, these are your choices. You must be patient as you wait for your blessings. Consider the farmers who eagerly look for the rains in the fall and in the spring. They patiently wait for the precious harvest to ripen. You, too, must be patient.

"And take courage. Don't grumble about your brother and sisters, or you will be judged in the same manner. You must also have patience in suffering, Grace. Great honor is given to those who endure under suffering.

"Now Grace, if you fail to follow these instructions you can expect these consequences at the end of your days—a bloody death. And you will be consumed by a great mountain of fire. And you will be surrounded by death and destruction. And those around you will be overcome by the fire and the smoke and burning sulfur.

"You must stop worshipping demons and idols made of gold, silver, bronze, stone, and wood—idols that neither see nor hear nor walk! And repent of your murders, or witchcraft or immorality or thefts.

"Do this Grace, and you, ever victorious, will have a pillar and place in my temple."

And Solon, Seraph and Jacob formed a circle around Grace to show their compassion, and comfort her, and show empathy for her. The blood in their hearts was pounding hard and their nostrils were wide open. And with their eyes opened wide and staring forward, they looked as if they were frozen together like one woman instead of four. Then Grace fell on her knees and wept. And the father turned his attention to his third child.

~~

"Solon, You are very wise and your strength lies in your understanding. Your understanding reaches far even throughout this solar system to the seven stars where you have the ability to walk among them. You are the sevenfold spirit connected to the seven stars. You have planned and fought many battles and gained the victory. You are a martyr for my word and for being faithful in your witnessing. There is a white robe waiting for you in my kingdom. But you must rest a little longer until the full number of your brother and sisters have been martyred.

"I know the things you do. I have seen your hard work and your patient endurance. I know you don't tolerate evil people. You have examined the claims of those who say they are apostles but are not. You have discovered they are liars. You have patiently suffered for me without quitting. You hate the deeds of the immoral, just as I do.

"And yet, Solon, I have this complaint against you. You don't love me or your siblings as you did at first. Look how far you have fallen from your first love! And, some of your deeds are far from right in the eyes of God. Go back to what you heard and believed at the first and turn to me again, work as you did at first.

"Whenever trouble comes your way, let it be an opportunity for joy. For when your faith is tested, your endurance has a chance to grow. So let it grow, for when your endurance is fully developed, you will be strong in character and ready for anything.

"If you want to know what you should do—ask, and I will gladly tell you. I won't resent your asking. But when you ask, be sure that you really expect an answer, for a doubtful mind is as unsettled as a wave of the sea that is driven and tossed by the wind. If you are indecisive, you should not expect to receive anything. You can't make up your mind. You waver back and forth in everything you do.

"And if you are poor, you should be glad. This is an honor for you. And if you are rich, you should be glad. For you have been humbled. In time, you will fade away like a flower in the field. The hot sun rises and dries up the grass; the flower withers, and its beauty fades away. So also, wealthy people will fade away with all of their achievements.

"If you patiently endure testing, you will be blessed. And afterward, you will receive the crown of life that you have been promised.

"And another thing, Solon, I know that you have great faith, but what's the use of saying you have faith if you don't prove it by your actions? That kind of faith can't save anyone. Suppose you see a brother or sister who needs food or clothing, and you say, "Well, good-bye and God bless you; stay warm and eat well"—but then you don't give that person any food or clothing. What good does that do? So you see, it isn't enough just to have faith. Faith that doesn't show itself by good deeds is no faith at all—it is dead and useless.

"Now someone may argue, 'Some people have faith; others have good deeds.' I say, 'I can't see your faith if you don't have good deeds, but I will show you my faith through my good deeds.' Do you still think it's enough just to believe in one God? Well, even the demons believe this, and they tremble in terror! Fool! When will you ever learn that faith that does not result in good deeds is useless? We are made right by what we do, not by faith alone. Just as the body is dead without a spirit, so also faith is dead without good deeds.

"And Solon, don't speak evil against your brother and sisters. If you criticize them and condemn them, then you are criticizing and condemning your father.

"And you are not a judge who can decide whether the commandments are right or wrong. Your job is to obey them. There is only one who can rightly judge among us. So what right do you have to condemn your neighbor?

"And finally, stop boasting about your own plans. All such boasting is evil. Remember, it is sin to know what you ought to do and then not do it."

"Now Solon, if you fail to follow these instructions you can expect these consequences. At the end of your days, your body will be filled with horrible, malignant sores and you will be plunged into darkness. And you will grind your teeth in anguish. And the trees you love will be burned, along with all of the grass. And for five months, you will endure a great agony like the pain of scorpion stings. And you will seek death but will not find it. You will long to die, but death will flee away!

"Now wake up! Strengthen what little remains for even what is left is at the point of death! Go back to what you heard and believed at the first and turn to me again and work as you did at first. Unless you do, I will come upon you suddenly as unexpected as a thief."

The father paused thoughtfully before looking into her face and when he spoke he had compassion in his voice.

"And yet, I know that you have not soiled your garments with evil deeds. And you will walk with me in white, for you are worthy. I will never erase your name from the book of life."

And Solon shuddered. And, Seraph, Jacob and Grace formed a circle around her to show their compassion, and comfort her, and show empathy for her. The blood in their hearts was pounding hard and their nostrils were wide open. And with their eyes opened wide and staring forward, they looked as if they were frozen together like one world instead of four. Then Solon fell on her knees and wept. He turned to Seraph, his youngest and smiled at her showing his pride.

~~

And finally, Seraph, whose eyes are bright like flames of fire. You have been given authority over one-quarter of the earth to defend the innocent with the sword against famine and disease and wild animals. You have stood at the altar and offered incense with the prayers of the saints. I know all of the things you do—your love, your faith, your service, and your patient endurance.

"But I have this complaint against you. You are permitting that woman, that Jezebel who calls herself a prophet—to lead my servants astray. She is encouraging them to worship idols, eat food offered to idols, and commit sexual sin.

"I gave her time to repent but she would not turn away from her immorality. Therefore, I will throw her upon a sickbed, and she will suffer greatly with all who commit adultery with her. Unless they turn away from all their evil deeds, I will strike her children dead."

Seraph understood clearly and she lowered her eyes in shame and began to weep. He continued to speak to her, sternly.

"Seraph, how can you claim that you have faith, if you favor some people more than others? For instance, suppose someone comes into your meeting dressed in fancy clothes and expensive jewelry, and another comes in who is poor and dressed in shabby clothes. If you give special attention and a good seat to the rich person, but you say to the poor one, 'You can stand over there, or else sit on the floor'—well, doesn't this discrimination show that you are guided by wrong motives? The poor in this world are rich in faith. They are the ones who will inherit the Kingdom. And yet, you insult the poor man! Isn't it your rich neighbor who oppresses you and drags you into court?

"And also, it is good when you truly love your neighbor as yourself. But if you pay special attention to the rich, you are committing a sin, for you are guilty of breaking that law. And the person who keeps all of the laws except one is as guilty as the person who has broken all of the commandments. The commandment that says, 'Do not commit adultery' also says, 'Do not murder'. So, if you murder someone, you have broken the entire law, even if you do not commit adultery.

"So whenever you speak, or whatever you do, remember that you will be judged by the law of love, the law that sets you free. For there will be no mercy for you if you have not been merciful to others. But if you have been merciful, then God's mercy toward you will win out over His judgment against you.

"And what is causing the quarrels and fights with your brother and sisters? Could it be that the whole army of evil desires are at war within you? Could it be that you want what you don't have, so you scheme and kill to get it? Are you jealous for what others have, and you can't possess, so you fight and quarrel to take it away from them?

"And yet the reason you don't have what you want is that you don't ask God for it. And even when you do ask, you don't get it because your whole motive is wrong—you want only what will give you pleasure. You adulterer. If your aim is to enjoy this world, you can't be my child. What do you think the Scriptures mean when they say that the Holy Spirit, placed within us, jealously longs for us to be faithful? You will gain more and more strength to stand against your evil desires. Humble yourself.

"Resist evil, my child, and it will flee from you. Wash your hands, and purify your heart, you hypocrite. Let there be tears for the wrong things you have done. Let there be sorrow and deep grief. Let there be sadness instead of laughter, and gloom instead of joy. When you bow down before the Lord and admit your dependence on Him, He will lift you up and give you honor.

"And if you choose not to follow these instructions, at the end of your days you can expect darkness and terror. You will hear my words but forget what you have heard. And that which you remember, you will not be able to write down. The secret will be kept just on the tip of your tongue. And death will follow you.

"But", the father said with a smile, "I have a different message for you if you have not followed this false teaching, these deeper truths. I will ask nothing more of you except that you hold tightly to what you have until my return. Because if you are victorious, and obey me to the very end, I will give you authority over all the nations. You will have the same authority I received from my Father, and I will give you the morning star!"

And Solon, Jacob, and Grace formed a circle around Seraph to show their compassion, and comfort her, and show empathy for her. The blood in their hearts was pounding hard and their nostrils were wide open. And with their eyes opened wide and staring forward, they looked as if they were frozen together as in one life instead of four. Then Seraph fell on her knees and wept.

~~

Then Solon spoke softly, while the others sobbed.

"Father, bless us. We were alone without instructions making our way. What must we do to gain your favor? Is there nothing left? Are we doomed to this fate?"

Then the father considered carefully before he answered.

"You each have a purpose and a way. This is your inheritance. Combine your strengths to ward off your weaknesses. Search yourself and you will have peace. But know that you can never have peace as long as truth stands alone."

"Father", Jacob cried. "Can a leopard change his spots? What hope have we to bind ourselves to one another? We are so different. It is impossible."

"At first it will seem this way, it is true. But you are living beings with a natural selection. And if each of you heeds my specific warning to you, you will control the forces inside you and gravitate towards each other, and find each other and become peaceful as the first day. You will discover that you are unified without great effort. Even as I speak, your bodies and minds have begun the process of adaptation. You are growing with what you have learned today, and changing your minds and spirits. You each will learn a lesson before you find the final solution. But the change in you begins with truth.

"This I know you can do. This you must do if you are to survive the final judgment and be at peace. And know that you can never have peace as long as truth stands alone. Who will stand with truth?"

They looked at each other not understanding his meaning. Then Grace asked a question.

"But father tell us, how do we begin? I can change myself but how can I help the others and reinforce your message to us? Where can we look for the answers we need?"

And Seraph added.

"Yes, we need to know how we should treat one another so that we can all be on one accord."

~~

The father rose and stretched and crept toward the bed that lay undisturbed, made well. He spoke.

"I will give you the key to decipher the code but first I must rest."

He lay down his head and after having adjusted his feet he slept. In the morning, he opened his eyes and began to speak to them.

~~

"Jacob, it is far easier to tear down a house than to build one up. Think of others at least as much as you think of yourself. The past is the past. Go right to increase your strength for strength lies in pairs. Go left to find your weaknesses and there you will find the one who truly loves you. The one, whom you admire so much, despises your ways. Stay clear of her or she will cut you down. The one you judge to lack intelligence loves you and is wise. Listen to her. Stop trying to change her, enslave her. Accept her for the unique person that she is. The one you ignore needs you. Be kind to her. She will save you when your tongue gets you into trouble.

"Grace, listen to your heart, not your friends. You know the answer for yourself. Go right to increase your wisdom for wisdom grows in pairs. Go left to find your weaknesses and there you will find the one who truly admires you. The one you fight to impress with your knowledge and wealth, whose approval you seek has no interest in you. She does not value those things. The one you judge as incapable needs your strength. Be kind to him and stop trying to make him strong. Today it is not in his constitution. The one you think you mentor is wiser than you. Listen to her.

"Solon, you alone are always attractive, a gentle soul, seeking the truth. You conform to be what is required; you adapt to be faster or slower; haughty or humble. Seek yourself within yourself and once you know who you are, you will be free to be yourself with the others. The one who comes to you and is attracted to you will never understand your silence. Don't follow her if you are weak. You cannot control her. The one you ignore is plotting against you. Look up and behind you before you find yourself in trouble again. The one that needs you despises you. Make yourself available. Love him and chastise him before it is too late for him.

"Seraph, go right to increase your strength as strength comes in pairs. Go left to find your weakness. The one you defend is jealous of you. Stop trying to control him. The one you seek can only take you in small doses. Don't give too much. The one who needs your wisdom does not know it.

"This will help to train you until I can return."

~~

And when he had finished, he left them. And they looked silently from one to the other with furrowed brows wondering what it all meant.

Table 1.1—Biblical Excerpts

Jacob's Lament to Grace	Selected excerpts – Job 3
Grace Alone Weeping	Selected excerpts – Job 19, Job 14
Grace's Lament to Solon	Selected excerpts – Job 3
Jacob's Lament to Solon	Selected excerpts – Job 4, Job 5, Job 6, Job 31
Father's Admonishment to the Four Children	God's message to John concerning warnings to the seven churches arranged by the four profiles – Revelations 2 & 3 James' message to the seven churches arranged by the four profiles – James 1 - 5

PART TWO

Framing the Issues

ONE

The Construct

- The human struggle is a seasonal affair like the cycles that can be found in nature.

- Four types of human behaviour exist in the universe. Consider them as views, realities, how we see things. One (maybe two) of these four realities dictate what system a body of people will live within—political, social, financial, moral—based on a predetermined definition of reality that goes back to the first four. Right now, we are living in a season of unreality, which manifests itself in revenge, destruction and business disorder, chaos.

- The basis of the human struggle stems from the differences between the four types of behaviour.

- Each of us has all four types within us. Three of these these four behaviours rise to the surface unconsciously and control our thoughts, beliefs, words and deeds.

- The fourth type of behaviour, which is hidden or suppressed (due to fear or loathing), is the object of discontent and therefore subject to attack, disdain and criticism.

- The primary behaviour is of course, the strongest and the natural way of thinking. The secondary strength and third are sought after for their novelty and knowledge. This is true for all types except one—unreality—the first and the last on the wheel. It dominates and will confront and or gain strength from the one in front or the one behind as it suits its purposes.

- These four types of behaviour are fueled by the four forces that exist in the universe—weak force, strong force, gravity and electro-magnetism and are reflective of their properties.

Two

Examining Controversy

In this meaningless life of mine I have seen both of these: a
righteous man perishing in his righteousness, and a wicked man
living long in his wickedness.

Ecclesiastes 7:15

Everything in the whole world seems to boil down to one word—
relationships. My friend, my enemy; love or the lack thereof; strategic
allies, strategic enemies; friends and competitors; users and used. Out of
these relationships spring levels of conflict. These are created in our
minds.

Success is measured on what parents, friends, even onlookers and
judges value. It is simple to get lost in someone else's idea of success. It
is how we are raised. To leave home and return with material wealth will
please some. To return with degrees will please others. The line is
divided and often attaining one will not lead to the other. These things
that we value drive us to achieve or fail. This, too, is created in our
minds.

《》

Why are we here anyway? A person who is struggling cannot hold himself accountable for his actions. We revolve in a cycle of joy and pain, adversity and comfort. The world can be turning perfectly smoothly and bam! Something smacks us in the face, knocking us back, unexpected, threatening to destroy our livelihood and lives. At every moment, a theme of conflict is brewing. Why can't it be smooth all of the time? Why must we come down from the highs life has to offer? There are logical reasons that we all accept—this is how we grow, things change, life is not meant to be happy all of the time, I am being tested, he brought it upon himself.

But there must be a deeper meaning than these. So we look at people around us for the clues in behaviour. *Someone* is challenging the actions or beliefs of someone who is different from himself. *Someone* with different beliefs is shielding her face from harmful unfounded allegations—trying to live in peace.

What if *someone* is really *everyone*?

We examine life, moment by moment, looking for clues to the mystery and asking questions.How did the Nazi regime rise to power and slaughter one-quarter of the Jewish nation?

How did it come to be that Africans were sold into slavery by the thousands and killed when they would not bend and obey? Why was one-quarter of the world's population slaughtered during the Christian crusades? And also, one-quarter of the American Indians? Why were the so-called witches stoned to death by the hundreds? Surely, someone noticed the folly of these plans before they were implemented.

Closer to home, what forces would drive a mother to murder her children or a police officer to beat beyond recognition a citizen he has sworn to protect. The conscientious worker finds himself under attack without just cause. Children are killing themselves. The boss conspires to get rid of the worker and the worker seeks to discredit the boss. Surely, someone can see that these acts were senseless.

But, maybe not. One-quarter of the middle eastern population is being annihiliated right now!

No. Those leading the fight were and still are solidly convinced of the glory in their purpose. They easily convince those who would follow in the sanctity of the mission with promises of bread, glory, praise, wealth.

Yet, there can be no logical explanation that is good enough to compensate for this scale of folly, loss of life. The true explanation of the human struggle is hidden beneath a disguise of goodness. It is as it has been described in the visions of Ezekiel, Daniel and John in Revelations.

There seems to be someone, always in the background looking to expose some tidbit of news. It may be an accidental discovery or an intentional investigation. It could be a real situation that needs to be exposed. But just as often it is an imagined condition, a small view of reality, unsubstantiated by truth and full of speculation, misunderstanding. The judgment errors and the large sins are treated with equal voracity. They are exposed for the world to see—if not the whole world, then certainly the immediate environment—the office, the church, the family. When tormenting the accused does not benefit the whole, it looks a lot like persecution. Persecution disrupts lives. Persecution breaks the spirit.

Throughout the world and in our work and home lives, conflict is a recurring theme. How can we learn to trust each other? What's the point of it all? What is the purpose of living except to work and eat, sleep and begin again and through it all, be persecuted by those who don't understand us—who disagree with our beliefs? Every person arrives at the point where the answers to these questions compel him to seek out, to know. Are we all destined to struggle in a life full of controversy?

There is friction in nearly every facet of life whether we are pushing or pulling, or rolling with the flow. The very word conjures up a negative image, but friction is not necessarily a bad thing. Friction compels us to create, to achieve, to find a better way or progress to the next level. Is it no wonder that we experience friction in all of our relationships? Getting started is usually the hardest part but once we move past the beginning point, momentum takes over and we can reach a goal quickly.

Pick any point since the beginning of time. There is a war looming in the background or there is a full war in the forefront. The landscape is littered with wrecked lives, destroyed structures and bodies of innocent victims. Look for the villains. They are oddly missing from the scene. As you look over the carnage searching for them, let me remind you again that the goal of war is peace. Peace is a hope that cannot be fully realized until there is an understanding and full respect for the total nature of humankind. But the full understanding does not come to us naturally. It must be learned.

As an individual, we can only see one part—our view. The truth is hidden behind *we* and *they*. The circle must be turned in order for the full span of the picture to be exposed. Once it is turned, we will come to know that there is no *they*. Only *we* exist.

Every day, people fight for religious freedom and more. Freedom to live in the lifestyle we choose; power, civil liberties, unborn babies and the continued existence of life. We are separated by what we see with our eyes and what we see with our eyes, we believe. The ideals that separate us are fraught with friction. On the surface, the reason for this conflict seems obvious. But the conflict has very little to do with the color of our skin, our bank accounts, our gender, the vices to which we are drawn or our religious affiliation. These external causes mask our true selves. It is a simple matter to attack a person because of his race or gender or religious affiliation or social sect. These conditions are obvious and can easily be seen by anyone. But they are not who we are. That which separates us is the darkest part of ourselves fueled by the microparticles and macroparticles of which all humans are comprised.

Understanding and accepting this ideal means that it doesn't matter if you are male or female, black, brown, red or yellow, parent or child, husband or wife, company leader or employee. You will know that the enemy is closer than you think and far less obvious than the color of his stripes. You will know why the educated scoff at the strong, why the bully harasses the weak, why the hero always gets the girl and why the brilliantly creative are always misunderstood.

Consider the animals of the wild. Their labor is to fill their bellies and repopulate their species in an infinite circle of life. Cannot mankind, the intelligent species, draw some conclusions about living in harmony from these? Have we advanced so far in our bid for technology that we cannot turn back to what is right and good?

We have all played one or more of the four roles in a classic conflict. In every major conflict (those leading to war whether private or professional), there must be a villain, a victim, a hero and a mediator. The villain oppresses, the victim is tormented, the hero uses ingenuity to resolve the conflict and the mediator arrives from nowhere with empathy and protection for the naive. Which part was played by whom is based on our reality. This is the human condition—the circle of human life.

But, what if the conflict model we live by is a hoax? What if there was no victim, or villain? What would happen to the hero and the mediator? What if we are all victims, and villains, heroes and mediators? Who says we have to be one or the other?

《》

Before I begin to lay out the evidence, I want to make sure that you understand my intent. This construct is a probability equation.

1. It has no bearing on intelligence. Behaviour and intelligence are two separate issues.

2. I am not a soothsayer, prophet or psychologist and this puts me in a precarious position with the theologist, the scientist and the psychologist. But I believe that what is written here will take the reader

a long way toward understanding the cyclic patterns of thought. I feel strong in this because of the way in which it was revealed to me. If it suits your idea of truth, then so be it. If not, forgive me for stumbling and correct me. The onus is on all of us to discover the truer answer.

PART THREE
Building The Construct

ONE

The Substratum of Everything

But God chose the foolish things of the world to shame the
wise; God chose the weak things of the world to shame the
strong. He chose the lowly things of this world and the despised
things—and the things that are not—to nullify the things that
are, so that no one may boast before him.

1 Corinthians 2:27-29

Ancient civilizations concluded that natural and earthly phenomena
were controlled by spirits with unpredictable human emotions. With
these ideas firmly entrenched in societal belief systems, sacrifices were
offered to natural objects—rivers, mountains, stars, the sun and moon
who were believed to be gods. Physical science has deciphered that this
natural phenomena is governed by laws—the sun always rises in the
east and sets in the west, the planets follow precise paths across the sky,
which can be predicted with a high degree of accuracy. Once the patterns were exposed and the universal laws applied, it was easy for mod-
ern man to see the folly of the ancients.

Look how far we have come from the days of worshipping idols and
natural phenomena and the practice of sacrificing humans. Could it be

that we are we still engaged in these same practices just in a more obscure form?

The substratum of all life lies within the collective unconscious of the human psyche. We are all in effect part of a dynamic mental engine that passes from person to person and from lifetime to lifetime through a medium that is much bigger than this universe. I call this medium God, but he is called by many names.

In the whole of human history, in the present times and no doubt in the future, the human experience is constructed on layers of four ideals—cause, reality, truth and clairvoyance. Nations rise up and are cut down or maintained based on these four ideals. Lives are reduced to ashes based on cause, wars are won based on reality, peoples are unified based on truth and societies continue to thrive and grow because of the mysteries of clairvoyance. To understand my meaning, it is important to establish a common understanding of these four terms, as I am certain that the images evoked will vary from person to person.

Sir Arthur Stanley Eddington, *(1882 to 1944)* a British astronomer, developed definitions for four terms—reality, cause, science and mysticism—while he was working on mathematical research for the theory of relativity. In his work, *The Nature of the Physical World,* Eddington uses inferential concepts from science and applies them to the human experience. The definitions he developed for reality, cause, science and mysticism helped to establish the basic foundation for the four terms used in this construct—cause, reality, truth and clairvoyance.

Cause

Cause (for the purpose of this construct) is unconditional antagonism; nothing preceded it, yet everything follows it. In this sense, cause is not retaliation, revenge or payback. It is the chicken that just happened before the egg was laid. It is two-dimensional and subtle, uncomplicated. It is *knowledge* learned by which everything is *judged*. It is *resolute*.

To understand cause, mathematicians measure relation, ratio, and knowledge of the pace of change. These are expressed in the formula—X is determined by Y, which at once reacts on X, and so Y finds itself depending on the new X. Colloquially expressed it would read—the date of the picnic will be determined by the weather forecast, which when known will determine the date of the picnic. The relation of effect to cause is commonly known as the reason.

In the human experience, cause is always expressed by change. Change frequently influences much more than the events, things or people targeted. Cause begins the chain of events and the resulting change then becomes the source of momentum.

Cause is imperceptible due to the slow moving and rhythmic events of life, which lull us into a false calm of stability. This is true for America. This is true for many countries.

I tried to think of something that was out of the range of change; where cause is not a factor. It would have to be something absolutely stable, and resistant to improvement or friction. Since the natural world is continuing to evolve and adapt, I could think of nothing. Nothing manmade is absolutely stable. In fact, many man made objects are positively fragile. But, it is this fragility that encourages progress, change, and the notion to build a better mousetrap.

Then I considered words—history, knowledge, philosophy, the Bible for example. Since its inception, many have tried to improve it, alter its interpretation but still it remains constant in the world. Anchored in time.

Then I realized that there is one other item that has not been affected by cause. It is the ideal of morality, ethics. Morality has not been affected by cause because it is the very basis of cause, the first cause. The answer to what *ought* to be done in various situations is a discussion that began with the first man and the debate rages on to this day. Philosophical reasoning is based on morality, and morality is the basis of religion.

Morality is behaving as you were taught to behave from infancy. Those who don't behave are punished. It is thinking as you have been brought up to think, to ignore what is natural within you, to conform to a set of values created by cause. To be moral means that you obey the traditional edicts of your community without hesitation or discussion, to conserve your natural instincts and follow the master plan, the first plan.

In cause, there is a mutual dependence between actions and reactions. In the human experience, cause is resolute, faithful. It is a set course of action created without any external motivation. It is steadfast and constant, bent and determined.

A man decided to purchase a home for himself and his son. He was certain that he would get financing, so about thirty days before the closing, he moved his belongings and his son into the house. He did not tell the owners that he was moving in. He simply made a key and moved in. A week before the closing, he found out that he was not eligible for financing and another buyer was waiting for the property. The owners went to meet the new buyer to show the house and found that the man and his son had moved in. They were shocked and angry. They wanted to sue him for rent. The father, his son and all of their belongings were thrown into the street. The father complained about his ill treatment and blamed the owners for his situation, citing them as the cause of his troubles.

Does the cause of this man's trouble lie within the owners of the property or within himself? No matter what your view of the final reaction, the first cause began with the father's decision. The decision, which was simple enough, came from within himself.

A strong causal stance is often evident by what life has to offer in the material world, the things that bring comfort and prestige. From the outside looking in, it is often called capitalism.

Reality

Reality is the physical proof of existence, which has been established through our senses—hardness, color, scent, volume of sound and flavor. Using our internal sense impressions, we project what we see, hear, taste, smell and feel to the external world. And these are recorded as pleasurable or painful. In this way, reality interprets and judges whether we see the glass as half full or half empty.

Reality seeks proof through investigation. It is that which *follows the nose* to find the answers. With reality, the senses are able to detect, learn and appreciate both the rewards and consequences of pleasure and pain. It is three-dimensional and more complicated than cause because for reality, *knowledge* depends not only on memory but also on *comparisons*. Comparisons lead to values and *judgment*. Is it true or false? Is it good or bad?

Reality recognizes that pain and pleasure are part of the same experience. So it works hard, and thrives on suffering believing that pleasure will be the reward.

Reality evokes emotion, loud cheers or tears. When we see the baby take his first steps, everyone is glad. And when our parents pass on, we wail aloud trying to keep them with us. It is only natural. To suppress it makes us feel ill inside and we can literally become ill when we repress our feelings.

Reality changes from person to person based on our collection of values and beliefs. It is bound up in judgment of whether or not it is true or is deserving of the emotion that it is designed to evoke. Reality is often the majority vote, without truth, and deeply rooted in the physical world. And as we contemplate nature, we cease to analyze the world and are conscious of the impressiveness of the whole.

This definition is no doubt different from what has been inferred through our experiences. The word reality is so often used interchangeably with words like solid, absolute and truth. They are completely different. Solid, absolute and truth are idioms, which denote factual proof with some probability of recurring i.e. the sun will rise in the east and set in the west. There is no value judgment involved. If you decide that, we are in the rainy season because it rained yesterday, and because you see the rain falling again today, then you have made a value judgment and given your opinion. Whether we are actually in the rainy season or not, still remains to be proven.

Reality sees, feels, touches, tastes and hears what is on the surface. Underneath the surface, things are often very different from what they seem. And because reality changes from person to person, it is *relative*, speculative and instinctive. It has no boundaries and can be fatal.

Truth

Truth is the result of the formation of ideas, the result of reasoning. It is not a static property, which is inherent in the idea. Truth happens to an idea. It becomes true. An idea is made true by the events that prove it.

In science, truth is the stark reality. It is five-dimensional. It puts a *value* on *knowledge*, remembers and *compares* it with new knowledge, *judges* it and *assigns* a more concise value on the combined knowledge and finally *sends* it out into the universe to see if it comes back as truth.

Truth comes to be based on external survey and is engineered to stand the test of time. If it does not stand the test of time, it is flexible enough to bow down to a better expression of truth.

It is numbers and facts calculated and recalculated in the metric symbols of the mathematician. It is tested and retested by the tools of the physicist to ensure the concreteness of the results. Truth is the precision of the laws of life. But life would be limited if we could feel no hope in the world around us beyond that which can be weighed and measured.

In the human experience, truth is beauty and light. I contemplated this as I looked out of my second story office window. The treetops were conducting a meeting in the sky with electric wires and power poles. I had a strong desire to taste the wind moving through those trees, wrap my arms around the trunks, and feel their strength. These too were truth and in an oddly calming way, beauty. It was evidence of nature and man living together.

The scientist often tears down reality to get past the senses to the heart of the truth. In doing so, he desensitizes his brain to the senses. He is not aware of pain or pleasure. The only purpose of touch, smell, feel, taste or sight is to reach the end game, to find the truth. This gives him pleasure. And yet, the mind still creates its own diversions, wandering here and there, searching through a fog of illusion.

Truth speaks in symbols—metrical, musical, hieroglyphical, and artistic. In this way, reasoning is applicable to symbolic knowledge while truth puts ideas into the proper perspective. It is original, influenced by and bound to nature. It is the very idea of God drawing us close as truth has strong connections to the spiritual world.

Truth, like the ox, moves slowly, stays focused and is a workhorse. Truth unifies people. Without truth, life is meaningless.

Clairvoyance

Clairvoyance refers to the capacity to perceive an idea through an extrasensory perception (intuition) whose result is absolute, unlimited and without restrictions or exceptions. The ideas, then, are perfect in quality and in nature, pure. It cannot be proven or disproved. It is conjured in the mind.

In the human experience, clairvoyance is unreality. It is four-dimensional. It puts a *value* on *knowledge*, remembers and *compares* it with new knowledge, *judges* it and *sends* it out into the universe as truth.

Clairvoyance has long been associated with evil spirits mostly because it is not easily understood. And when it has been observed through the eyes of cause and reality, it is frightening and illogical. It conjures up pictures of Rumpelstilskin and trolls living beneath bridges; witches casting spells, supernatural phenomena that cannot be explained by science. It is in fact a great mystery that God has left us, the inconstant variable, little known and warily understood.

It is the sixth sense, the intuitive power that cannot be perceived by the five senses—touch, smell, feel, see and hear. Where the five senses evoke images of reality and emotions, the sixth sense evokes a sense of unreality. Like reality, it cannot be proven as truth since it has strong ties to the spiritual world outside of the observable universe.

Spiritualism, unlike religion, is personal and intimate contact with God. We all have the ability to talk directly to Him and know that He will answer us. But somehow, this idea became associated with evil rather than good. It is a natural and undeniable part of ourselves.

It is knowledge that is both personal and private. It does not submit to systematic order or analysis. It is that which guides us into our connection with God. It comes spontaneously when we spread out our hands to Him and to those who need our help. It does not come through self-examination, study or deep reflection of ourselves.

These spiritual feelings of clairvoyance, are made up of emotions, purpose and values stored in our consciousness. Through clairvoyance, we are closer to nature and therefore creative and lighthearted in our approach to life.

To deny, ignore or refute this spiritual force within you is like waiving your rights to a soul. True joy becomes a deficiency to be pitied like a man without a sense of humor.

《》

We live by laws—moral laws, laws of nature, physical laws and spiritual laws. They were drafted by people whose main ideal and purpose was derived from one of the four definitions—cause, reality, truth or clairvoyance. Societies have risen and fallen based on these laws. The laws are not arbitrary. We are all subject to them or influenced by them.

Two

Life's Unconscious Nature

And in the fire was what looked like four living creatures. In appearance, their form was that of a man, but each of them had four faces and four wings. Their legs were straight; their feet were like those of a calf and gleamed like burnished bronze.

Under their wings on their four sides, they had the hands of a man. All four of them had faces and wings, and their wings touched one another. Each one went straight ahead; they did not turn as they moved.

Their faces looked like this: Each of the four had the face of a man, and on the right side had the face of a lion and on the left the face of an ox; each also had the face of an eagle.

Ezekiel 1:5-10

When I was a child, I was easily persuaded to play a game called *paper, rock, scissors.* (If you are not familiar with the game, ask your children. This would be a good excuse to talk to them.) Briefly, the game has three rules—paper covers rock, rock breaks scissors and scissors cut paper—an endless circle. The game to this day has no appeal for me because there seemed to be no point. Winning, (if you call it winning) was a factor of mental alertness and to a lesser degree, cleverness. Since I was neither alert nor clever, I considered it a game of chance. When I asked the children what the point of the game was they told me it was "a *decision making game*", "a *dispute resolution game*" and "a *game of elimination*". When I visualized the game later, I realized that *paper, rock, scissors* is an illustration of the continuous cycle of Ezekiel's wheel.

Humans are more than a bundle of arbitrary sensory impressions. We are beings with purpose and responsibilities. God has given us visions so that we know what we are supposed to do, when it must be done and how it must be done. These visions are available to anyone who is open to it, has faith and believes.

Ezekiel was a Jewish priest whose visions were recorded from 593 B.C. to 571 B.C. More than any other prophet whose writings appear in the Bible, his visions and prophecies have been dated with precision. Like many of the prophets of the day, he prophesied in politically volatile times, similar to the times we live in now. His visions, like many, were difficult to understand, bewildering, communicated during the night and recorded for the benefit of the people. An interesting thing about visions is that they are often seen multiple times and by more than one person. Many receive the message, but only a few will hear it.

On the surface, the vision he described in chapter one of the book Ezekiel appears to be symbolic, an unearthly vision of God's awesome power manifest in a grotesque creature with four separate heads. This creature has been interpreted as a representative of the divine. The whole chapter appears to be written in abstract poetry, theatrics. But if you strip away the obvious religious interpretation of the divine, you will find the functional description of the four purposes of mankind— cause, reality, truth and clairvoyance—with significant pointers to the redemption and unification of man. These four purposes fit well with

---

1   See Table 3.1—1 Corinthians 12:1-12

the spiritual gifts that God has given us—knowledge, faith, wisdom and the power to heal.[1]

The notion of these four ideals begins in the beginning of biblical history where a river watering the garden flowed from Eden. And from Eden, it separated into four rivers. The first is Pishon which winds through Havilah where there is gold. (The gold of this land is good; aromatic resin and onyx.) The second is Gihon, which winds through the entire land of Cush. The third is the river Tigris that runs along the east side of Asshur and the fourth river is the Euphrates.[2] Here in the beginning, the four were pure, and good.

When we see the four together again, they are described by Ezekiel, then by Daniel[3] and finally by John[4] in Revelations. Each of these prophets saw the four living beings in visions. And others continue to see them to this day. But, after the beautiful scene in the garden, the forms are no longer pure and good like the rivers from which they flowed. Now they take the shape of four separate living beings, equal with four distinct forms and purposes that are consistent throughout the Bible.

In his vision, Ezekiel saw four separate living beings with four different faces; a pair of legs each, a pair of human hands each and four wings each, a monster. The wings of each living being touched the wings of two others. The living beings were able to fly in any direction chosen without turning around. Each of the four beings was perched on wheels and inside each wheel was a smaller wheel. Each of the four beings had a spirit and the spirit was in the wheels. All four wheels looked the same; each wheel had a second wheel turning crosswise within it. They went in whatever direction the spirit chose, and they moved straight forward in all directions without having to turn around. The living beings looked like bright coals of fire or brilliant torches, and it looked as

---

2   Four Rivers of Paradise (Genesis 2:10)
3   Daniel 7:1.
4   Revelations 4:6

though lightning was flashing back and forth among them. And the living beings darted back and forth like flashes of lightning. When the living beings moved, the wheels moved.

《》

This vision was interpreted for me as the four-dimensional mind of mankind. Each of the four has separate and distinct purposes, and yet we are aware of all four types because each of the four resides in each of us. This is demonstrated by each of the four having four heads and by the wheel inside the wheel. Plato and Jung discussed the idea of the four-dimensional mind.[5] Freud documented the construct of a three dimensional mind.[6] So, it is no surprise that in Ezekiel's vision one of the four beings stood alone. In the wheel, it is the one that is out of the line of sight, the hidden spoke that is missing from plain view. "One, two, three—but where, my dear Timaeus, is the fourth...?"[7] Plato wrote about 425 B.C. in his work Timaeus. It illustrates the idea that each of us has a fourth characteristic that is hidden or seldom used.

That the being can fly in any direction without turning around, says that we all have a dominant character and purpose that takes over and suppresses the lesser characteristics. There is no conflict within us about our assigned purpose. The wheels are a redundant depiction of the same idea. In the outer wheel are our true selves, our dominant character; in the inner wheel are all four of the ideals, which we all possess.

The bright coals of fire, lightning, darting here and there are matter particles; atoms fueled by the four forces of the universe—weak force, strong force, gravity and electromagnetism. These four forces exist in the microparticles and macroparticles of which we are all comprised.

---

5   Jung, *Psychology and Religion*
6   Freud, *Civilization and its Discontents*
7   Plato, Timaeus

These rise up when we charge them through our thoughts and the result is our emotions. But, these charges are controllable if we choose to control them[8].

The four types have repeated in a quaternal birth pattern since the first four.

---

8   They went in whatever direction the spirit chose. Ezekiel 1:12

Table 3.1—Lunar Dates and Profiles

From			To			
Month	Day	Year	Month	Day	Year	Profile
2	5	1647	1	24	1648	Philosopher
1	25	1648	2	10	1649	Warrior
2	11	1649	2	9	1650	Unifier
2	1	1650	1	20	1651	Mediator
2	16	1999	2	4	2000	Philosopher
2	5	2000	2	23	2001	Warrior
1	24	2001	1	11	2002	Unifier
2	12	2002	2	9	2003	Mediator
2	1	2003	2	21	2004	Philosopher
1	22	2004	1	8	2005	Warrior
2	9	2005	2	28	2006	Unifier
1	29	2006	1	17	2007	Mediator

It is the background, the wallpaper of who we are. It is why we do what we do. With each new generation, these four types have become hidden in our cultural differences, our environment and social values. The environment and influences, upbringing, make us uniquely and individually who we are; while collectively, we are told who we should be based on the strongest force of the four. But the four have not changed. These four are manifested in our every day life and are the basis for the conflict between us not the external characteristics that we see—skin color, male and female, parent and child. But, don't take my words as the gospel. Study it for yourself.

Table 3.2—Forms and Functions

Forms and Functions	Cause	Reality	Truth	Clairvoyance
Heads - Ezekiel 1	Human	Lion	Ox	Eagle
Placement - Ezekiel 1	Front	Right	Left	Back
Sound - Ezekiel 1	Like the voice of the Almighty.	Like the tumult of an army.	Roar of rushing waters.	No sound.
Direction – Ezekiel	South – 10:3-8	North – 9:1-11	West – 13:1-23	East – 11:7-12
The Total Picture Ezekiel 1:27	From the waist down, he looked like fire.	Brilliant light surrounded him.	Waist up was like glowing metal.	Like the appearance of a rainbow – radiant.
Sources of Conflict – Ezekiel	10:2 – Fire from the wheels like burning coals scattered among the city.	8:5 – Idol of jealousy. 8:17 – Fill the land with violence. 9:2 – Each with a deadly weapon in his hand.	11:2 – Plotting and giving wicked advice. 11:8 – You fear the sword, conformed to the standards around you.	13:2,3 – False prophets, uttered lying divination, prophesy out of their own imaginations. Follows their own spirit, seeing nothing.
Equal to each other The Temple Area Ezekiel 40, 42:15-20	West Gate 500 cubits	North Gate 500 cubits	South Gate 500 cubits	East Gate 500 Cubits
Spiritual Gifts 1 Corinthians 1:1-12	He gives the gift of special knowledge.	The Spirit gives special faith to another.	To one person the Spirit gives the ability to give wise advice.	And to someone else he gives the power to heal the sick.
Messages to the Seven Churches Revelations 2	Pergamum The one who has a sharp two-edged sword. Laodicea The one who is the Amen – the faithful and the true witness, the ruler of God's creation.	Smyrna First and the Last, who died and is alive. Philadelphia One who is holy and true. The One with the key of David, who opens doors and no one, can shut them, who close doors that no one can open.	Ephesus The one who holds the 7 stars in his right hand and walks among the 7 gold lamp stands. Sardis The sevenfold spirit and the seven stars.	Thyatira Whose bright eyes are bright like flames of fire, whose feet are like polished bronze. The one who searches out the thoughts and intentions of every person.
Revelations 4:7	Man	Lion	Calf	Eagle

Four Realities

The four basic human types described in Ezekiel, in Daniel and again by John in Revelations can be described as the four different views of reality—resolute, relative, stark and unreality.

Table 3.3—Behaviour Model

Behaviour Model	Resolute Reality	Relative Reality	Stark Reality	Unreality
Ideals	Cause	Reality	Truth	Clairvoyance
Profile	Philosopher	Warrior	Unifier	Creative
Strength	Knowledge	Fight	Wisdom	Sight
Purpose	Teach	Defend	Unify	Support
Gains Understanding Through	Historical facts and mathematical equations.	Five senses – hear, see, touch, taste, smell	Patient observation and spiritual revelation	Creative mental imagery supported by historical precision

Resolute is driven by internal cause, relative is impelled by the senses, stark is compelled by the search for truth, and unreality is compelled by a need to protect and serve some aspect of life.

In each of these realities, one of the four is a major strength, one is a secondary strength, one is a weakness and one is hidden or ignored, feared. This is invariably true except in the case where a caregiver or strong influence possesses the hidden trait as a dominant trait. In this case, the hidden value may not be often used, but it would have surely been passed through. These four models are universal and up until the present, unchanging.

Resolute Reality

Resolute reality defines the world and teaches. It is the words of the philosopher, based in fact, which is both real and imagined. The philosopher's warnings come from an inbred fear—back to the days of the first man. Exacting laws, rules and warnings are a subset. When I think back to the first man, I imagine he must have felt some guilt, been kicking himself, for allowing the woman to persuade him, so he warns all of his subsequent generations by creating laws, teaching. Underneath these warnings, laws and lessons are the moral implications of not following the rules.

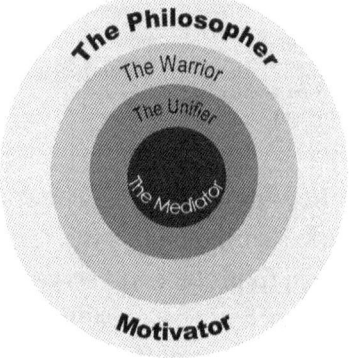

The philosopher is resolute because he makes decisions by consulting the facts he has learned. These have been passed down to him through his lineage and may no longer be true. But truth is less important than upholding tradition and accepted facts are not always true.

Once he has decided on a course of action, it is difficult for him to stop. Pride confuses sensibility, logic and reason. The philosopher's second strongest ideal is his senses, relative reality, which can lead to a violent and explosive nature when he is not getting his way. He becomes the impetuous child. He will listen to truth and understand it—if it is explained well and spoken in the language of facts. But listening, like truth, is his weakness. Truth comes too slowly and often conflicts with plans already in motion. Unreality is hidden. It reeks of forces he does not understand and fears. When I was researching this construct, I talked to several *philosophers'* who told me that in their youth, they prayed not to be the one who could hear voices. A prominent journalist made the same comment in a magazine recently. When I read it, I smiled.

In history and the present day, many famous men and women were born into resolute reality. I know this because the quaternal pattern repeats itself every four years as it has since the first man[9]. The brilliant, imaginative and the creatively evil are listed together in Table 3-4. Read their biographies[10] and you will begin to understand what I know to be true.

---

9 Based on the Lunar Calendar, not the Gregorian Calendar
10 MSN Search—Internet

Table 3.4—Resolute Reality, the Philosopher

Name	Birth	Profession	Known For
Adams, John Quincey	10/30/1735	Politician	President, Author of Declaration of Independence
Callas, Maria	12/04/1923	Soprano	Classical Italian Style
Clerk-Maxwell	06/13/1832	Physicist	Invented the Telescope
Cozzens, James Gould	08/19/1903	Philosopher	Literary and Military Career
Cukor, George	07/07/1899	Director	Gone With the Wind, 1939
Custer, General George	12/05/1839	Military Commander	Last Stand
Davis, Angela	01/27/1948	Civil Rights Activist	Political Activist - legendary
Edelman, Angela Wright	06/07/1943	Civil Rights Activist	Champion of Children's rights
Einstein, Albert	03/14/1879	Scientist	Theory of Relativity
Ford, Henry	07/30/1863	Inventor	Industrialist, Inventor
Gates, Bill	10/28/1955	Inventor	Founder of Microsoft
Giovanni, Nikki	06/08/1947	Author	Poet who helped define the conscience of a nation
Hindenburg, Paul von	10/02/1847	Military	President of Germany Appointed Hitler as Chancellor
Hitchcock, Sir Alfred	08/13/1899	Director	Popular TV Mysteries
Hobbes, Thomas	04/05/1588	Philosopher	Political, author, political theorist
Hubbard, L. Ron	03/13/1911	Author	Creator of Scientology
Hume, David	05/07/1711	Philosopher	Speculative, Historian
Jefferson, Thomas	04/13/1743	Politician	President, Author of Declaration of Independence
Johnson, James Weldon	06/18/1871	Poet	Novelist, Playwright
Keats, John	10/31/1795	Poet	Major Figure in the Romantic Movement
King, Stephen	09/21/1947	Author	Horror Novels and Movies
Mozart, Wolfgang Amadeus	01/27/1756	Classical Composer	Child Prodigy, Symphonies
Mussolini, Benito	07/29/1883	Politician	Dictator, Italy
Ness, Eliot	04/19/1903	Crime Fighter	Chicago Prohibition Bureau
Shakur, Tupac	06/17/1975	Philosopher - Rapper	Assassinated in his prime
Stalin, Joseph	12/09/1879	Dictator	Marxist Revolutionary
Stauffenberg, Claus	11/15/1907	Military – Nazi	The foiled assassination attempt of Hitler
Twain, Mark	11/30/1835	Author	U.S. Humorist and Lecturer
Whitman, Walt	05/31/1819	Poet	Revolutionary poetry dealing with very private experiences.

Relative Reality

Relative reality is the change maven—it organizes and improves. It is of the senses—that which we can see, hear, smell, touch, taste and intuit. It is the warrior, so named because of the highly competitive nature and the need to know / see what is real in order to decide the genuineness of it. What the philosopher has defined and teaches is questioned by the warrior.

Relative reality is often unsubstantiated—the gut feeling. Certainty is hard won through lessons, failures and success. Listening is a difficult chore but she is clever.

The success of the warrior, just as in war, depends on building a reciprocal relationship with allies, spies and supporters. She thrives on being surrounded by a small circle of people whom she loves and with whom she can compete.

The warrior has a strong sense of direction—relative reality. Her second strength is stark reality, truth, and she is always searching for it. Clairvoyance—unreality, is the weakest of the three. It is difficult to hear the voice of the spirit with so much chatter. She is annoyed by resolute reality—the philosopher. She has no patience to listen to monologues, facts, or what she perceives as boastful lies.

Many famous men and women were born into a relative reality and followed their noses throughout life. The fighting spirits, the losers and the winners are listed in Table 3.5.

Table 3.5—Relative Reality, The Warrior

Name	Birth	Profession	Known For
Arnold, Benedict	01/14/1741	Military	Traitor to the United States
Browning, Robert	05/07/1812	Poet	Book length poems with an emphasis on individual psychology
Capote, Truman	09/30/1924	Author	Flamboyant, southern author Novels - In Cold Blood, The Onion Field
Carter, Jimmy	10/02/1928	Politician	Habitat for Humanity Project
Chisholm, Shirley	12/01/1928	Politician	First Black Woman elected to congress
Dali, Salvador	05/11/1904	Painter	Surrealist Artist
Dunne, Dominick	10/29/1925	Journalist	Chilling stories about the rich and famous, Vanity Fair
Freud, Sigmund	05/06/1856	Scientist	Founder of Psychology
Giancana, Sam	05/24/1908	Mafia	Organized Crime Leader
Goering, Hermann Wilhelm	01/12/1893	Military	Nazi, Founded the Gestapo, set up concentration camps
Gotti, John	10/27/1940	Gangster	Teflon Don
Heydrich, Reinhard	08/04/1904	Military	Nazi, Over the Gestapo, Known as the hangman,
Himmler, Heinrich	10/07/1900	Military	Nazi, head of the SS, directed the Gestapo
Johnson, Lyndon	08/28/1912	U. S. President	Vietnam War
Keller, Helen	06/27/1880	Writer	Advocate for the deaf / blind
King, Martin Luther	01/15/1929	Civil Rights Activist	I Have a Dream
Lucas, George	05/14/1944	Director	Highly Imaginative, Star Wars
Nash, John Forbes	6/13/1928	Mathematician	Established the mathematical principles of games theory.
Nietzsche, Friedrich Wilhelm	10/14/1844	Philosopher	Speculative, Psychology
Nixon, Richard	01/09/1913	Politician	President, Watergate
Oppenheimer, J. Robert	04/22/1904	Scientist	Physicist, Father of the Atom Bomb
Roosevelt, Eleanor	10/11/1884	President's Wife	20th Century most influential and admired woman
Rousseau, Jean Jacques	06/28/1712	Philosopher	Political, author, political theorist, composer
Schopenhauer, Arthur	02/22/1788	Philosopher	Speculative
Shange, Ntozake	10/19/1952	Writer	Playwright, Novelist
Shaw, George Bernard	07/26/1856	Writer	Playwright, Novelist
Singleton, John	01/06/1968	Director	Writer – Boyz in the Hood
Stern, Isaac	07/21/1920	Musician	Violinist
Truman, Harry S.	05/08/1884	U. S. President	World War II
Warhol, Andy	08/06/1928	Artist	Campbell Soup Ads
Washington, George	02/22/1732	Military, Politician	First President
Watson, James Dewey	04/06/1928	Scientist	Geneticist

Stark Reality

Stark reality is truth. It is called stark because it is not sugarcoated. It is not vain. It is not puffed up. It is plain, unadorned and complete. It is scientific, precise and can be brutally painful to look at. It is what it is. It unifies and plans.

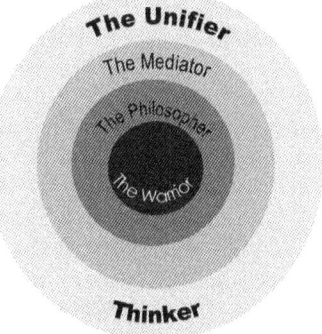

The one who responds with the true answer, has learned it through a life long and passive process. This phenomenon occurs without effort. Life begins slowly, in a low energy mind that is watching and listening, conforming as the face of truth changes. Wisdom is comprised of the highest probability of truth, which comes to be the absolute power required to unify people.

Truth changes and gives the ability to change. It cannot be bribed or coerced into less truth. It interprets the patterns of the world and describes the outcome in parables, stories and examples.

Stark reality ignores the whole world in pursuit of its goal. The second strength for the unifier profile is unreality, clairvoyance, a highly developed sense of spiritual union. Resolute reality, the philosopher, is the weakest link. The thoughts move much faster than words. The silent one avoids entrapment, ridicule and judgment from those who don't understand. Resolute reality—the warrior is hidden. There are ways—other than a physical war—to change things. Truth can end old conflicts but always begins new controversy.

The significant contributors and the unspeakable are listed in Table 3.6.

Table 3.6—Stark Reality, The Unifier

Name	Birth	Profession	Known For
Aaron, Hank	02/05/1934	Athlete	Baseball Player
Albright, Madeleine	05/15/1937	Politician	Secretary of State
Arafat, Yassar	08/24/1929	Palestinian Leader	Co-founder of the PLO
Berkowitz, David	06/01/1953	Convicted Murderer	Son of Sam
bin Laden, Osama	00/00/1957	Military Strategist	Militant Islamic Leader
Bonaparte, Napoleon I	08/15/1769	Military	Dictator, Emperor of France
Bradley, Ed	06/22/1941	Journalist	Co-editor of 60 minutes
Cochran, Johnny	10/03/1941	Defense Attorney	O. J. Simpson Case
Comte, Auguste	01/19/1798	Philosopher	Scientist, Sociologist, Founder of Positivism
Darwin, Charles Robert	02/12/1809	Philosopher	Science, Discoverer of Natural Selection
Ford, Gerald	07/15/1917	Politician	President
Gandhi, Mahatma Mohandas	10/02/1869	Civil Rights Leader	Fasted to protest religious persecution
Geronimo	06/12/1829	Indian Leader	Last to fall, brilliant strategist
Goebbels, Paul Joseph	10/29/1897	Military – Master proprogandist	Nazi, Hitler's enthusiastic supporter, a bitter anti-Semite
Griffin, Merv	07/06/1925	Talk Show Host	Hotel tycoon
Hawking, Stephen	01/08/1942	Scientist	Physicist
Hirohito, Showa Tenna	04/29/1901	Governing Ruler	124th Emperor of Japan
Hitler, Adolf	04/20/1889	Military	Dictator, Leader of the Nazi Movement
Hoffa, Jimmy	02/14/1913	Teamster Leader	Murdered
Holmes, Oliver Wendell	08/29/1809	Writer	Moral Maps
Hughes, Langston	02/01/1902	Writer	Brilliant poetry and plays
Kennedy, John Fitzgerald	05/29/1917	Politician	Assassinated President
Kierkegaard, Soren	05/13/1813	Danish Philosopher	Theologian, existentialism
Lee, Shelton Jackson (Spike)	3/20/1957	Director	Film, Writer
Malcolm X	5/19/1925	Civil Rights Activist	Assassinated Leader
Mandela, Nelson	04/02/1909	Civil Rights Activist	Jailed for his beliefs
Owens, Jessie	09/12/1913	Athlete	Track and Field Athlete
Picasso, Pablo	10/25/1881	Painter	Cubism
Powell, Colin	04/05/1937	Military	Secretary of State
Roosevelt, Franklin Delano	01/30/1882	Politician	President
Thatcher, Margaret	10/03/1925	Politician	Respected Prime Minister Great Britain
Von Bulow, Claus	04/10/1909	Businessman	Accused of attempting to murder his wife
Winfrey, Oprah	01/29/1954	Business Woman	Talk Show Host, Healer
Wright, Frank Lloyd	06/08/1869	Architect	Timeless, functional designs

Unreality

But it is the spirit in a man, the breath of the Almighty, that gives him understanding.

—Job xxxii. 8.

Unreality relates to all things spiritual and is the least understood of the four. Unreality is difficult to identify, quantify and to observe. But it is characteristically the mediator. It supports and defends.

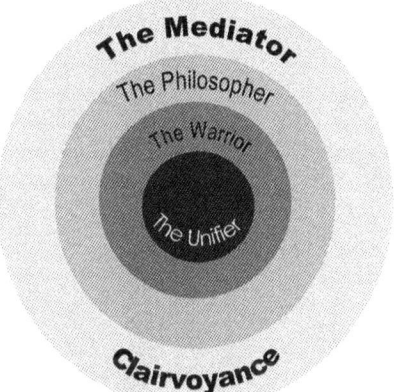

When I was researching this construct, more than one person told me that they found it hard to believe that everyone in their graduating class had the same qualities that they had. "Those people were nothing like me." This statement is true. It is true because in a normal state, without conflict, the face of unreality looks different on each clairvoyant person. Unreality is an ambiguous term. However, in a state of hostile conflict, at a high energy level, the mediators all behave in essentially only one way. They attack. They become the tyrant, the accuser and judge with whom no one can reason. And as they attack, they gain strength, getting stronger and stronger until they are in a position to win through intellect or brute force. On the other hand, when the mediator is under attack, they keep a cool head. They do the opposite of what you expect. And when they are feeling hurt or saddened—whether displaying empathy for others or themselves—they cry.

The mediator has sworn an oath, signed a pact; to serve justice to the unjust, to deliver those who are in bondage and to avenge at all costs and by any means. When they choose a course to deliver on this promise, it is not arbitrary. They are thoroughly convinced that their course is for the noblest of causes. Mediators have the power to rescue or to destroy.

The second strength for this profile is resolute reality—the philosopher—well-read, well-spoken. Relative reality—the warrior—is hardly a weakness, but still it plays only a minor role since the mediator wins by her wits, knowledge and verbal skills. The enemy of clairvoyance is truth, which is hidden in the mediator profile. The mediator will not listen to truth in a high-energy state.

In history and the present day, many famous men and women were born into unreality. The empathetic defenders and the unreasonable judges are listed in Table 3.7.

Table 3.7—Unreality, The Mediator

Name	Birth	Profession	Known For
Beethoven, Ludwig van	12/16/1770	Classical Composer	Pianist, Genius
Brown, John	1800	Abolitionist	Led a violent crusade against slavery
Bush, George Jr.	07/07/1950	President	War on Terrorism
Capone, Al	01/17/1899	Gangster	Scarface
Chopin, Frederic	02/22/1810	Composer	Pianist
Clinton, Bill	08/20/1950	Politician	President
Davis, Miles	05/25/1926	Musician	Jazz Trumpeter
Dershowitz, Alan M	1938	Attorney	Defended Claus Von Bulow and won
Dickerson, Emily	12/10/1830	Poet	Classical and Timeless
Dillinger, John	06/28/1902	Gangster	Bank Robber
Eddington, Sir Arthur Stanley	12/28/1882	Scientist	Astronomer
Eisenhower, Dwight D.	10/14/1890	Politician	President
Eliot, T. S.	09/26/1888	Poet	British Playwright and critic
Flynt, Larry	11/01/1942	Journalist	Men's Entertainment Literature
Frost, Robert	03/26/1874	Poet	Pulitzer Prize Winner for the work New Hampshire
Hefner, Hugh	04/09/1926	Journalist	Men's Entertainment Literature
Hegel, Georg Wilhelm Friedrich	08/27/1770	Philosopher	Political, Idealist - Phenomenology
Hess, Rudolph	04/26/1894	Military	Nazi Leader, Occultist
Hoover, J. Edgar	01/01/1895	Military	FBI Director
Hoover, Herbert	08/10/1874	Military	President
Jackson, Michael	08/30/1962	Singer	King of Pop
Jung, Carl	07/26/1875	Scientist	Psychiatrist
Klein, Calvin	11/19/1942	Fashion Designer	Fashion Designer
Locke, Alain Le Roy	04/25/1886	Philosopher	First Black Rhodes Scholar
Marx, Karl	05/05/1818	Philosopher	Political, Philosopher, Economist
Newton, Isaac	01/04/1643	Scientist	Physicist, Mathematician
Queen Latifa	03/18/1970	Singer	Singer, actor
Reagan, Ronald	02/07/1915	Politician	President
Rice, Condoleeza	11/15/1958	Politician	Keen Foreign Policy Strategist
Schultz, Charles	11/26/1922	Artist	Creator of Charlie Brown
Schwartzkopf, Norman	1934	Commander	Desert Storm
Spielberg, Steven	12/18/1946	Director	Director, Writer, Producer
Stravinsky, Igor	06/17/1882	Composer	Violinist

《 》

In the normal course, these four types are not in conflict. They learn from each other. Each of the four has a different general purpose and all four are required for the continued survival of life on earth, balance. These different purposes bind the four together in an unspoken state of cooperation. But… ignore the hidden spoke in the wheel for too long and conflict will surely emerge. Silence is the beginning of every struggle.

When we consider Ezekiel's wheels turning clockwise, it's not hard to imagine taking the best of what is in front of us. What we can see, we can learn from and imitate. It is also not difficult to visualize the wheels stopping, and as you look backward, you see what you fear behind you. You fear that which is hidden and come to know that the one chasing you is looking to resolve some conflict with you.

Paper covers rock, rock breaks scissors and scissors cut paper. The philosopher fears clairvoyance and seeking help to defend himself, he runs to the warrior but the warrior is not there. She is pursuing the unifier to learn the secrets of her silence. But the unifier has left to question clairvoyance as the missing piece in her search for truth. And we are back where we began—the clairvoyant mediator is off chasing the philosopher looking for knowledge or simply a good debate. Each spoke in the wheel gains in strength what is lacking from the ones ahead as far as can be seen.

In the opposite direction, the direction of conflict, the unifier (truth) tears down reality (the warrior) because the senses can be deceiving. The warrior wrestles with cause (the philosopher) because cause wants to bind up the world in rules. The philosopher condemns clairvoyance (the mediator) and discredits her to weaken her spirit. And the mediator does not identify with the ways of truth (the unifier). The lack of observable empathy and slow responses look suspiciously like warning signals—so she judges her to be inconsiderate and sometimes incompetent. And the mediator may state her opinion about this perceived problem to anyone who will listen.

Out of this chaos comes unity—as everyone is eventually forced to reconcile their ideals to the truth. And all of these thoughts and actions are charged by the forces that give rise to the matter particles within us.

THREE

Atom and the Four-Dimensional Mind

And we know that in all things God works for the good of those
who love him, who have been called according to his purpose.
For those God foreknew he also predestined to be conformed to
the likeness of his Son, that he might be the firstborn among
many brothers. And those he predestined, he also called; those
he called, he also justified; those he justified, he also glorified.

What then can we say in response to this? If God is for us, who
can be against us?

Romans 8:28-31

Wallpaper intrigues me. Some of the patterns are complex and mul-
tifaceted while others are decidedly simple. I have stayed in a few hotels
across the globe and have studied the wallpaper patterns with great
interest. At first glance, the pattern is hardly noticeable. But then, I have
a tendency to look up from my laptop towards the ceiling, and think.
And that is when I begin to detect the pattern, the flaws in the pattern,

and where the edges connect. I know what you're thinking. "Get a life." I will. Right now, I have a purpose.

My study of human behaviour began in a similar way. One day I announced without deliberation that I was going to write a book on archetypes. This seemed to be my purpose and I wasted no time beginning my task. Subconsciously, I had been studying the effect of different types of people on my mood and my influence on the moods of others. It turned into a study on racism in the workplace for which I collected quite a lot of data. As I reviewed the outcomes, I realized that certain types of people rubbed me the wrong way consistently, or the same types disliked me consistently, and it did not matter what race they were or their income.

Throughout my early years, I felt as if I were a target for sabotage. The villains could be both male and female of a certain type; black or white did not matter. They were equally suspicious of me. With this information, I surmised that the obvious and external properties of a human are unimportant elements in defining the causal relationship in a conflict. All of my data came down to one line—*they were born to mistrust me.* Then I wondered if they were born to be suspicious of everyone. Who would know?

I searched for why we behave the way we do knowing somehow that the four forces were involved but other than metaphorically, I could not quite connect them to human behaviour. I asked questions of doctors, mystics, psychologists, scientists, and they seemed to have no idea of my meaning or direction. At one point, I laughed thinking that it must be a government cover-up.

My friend Nita gave me the Stephen Hawking book *A Brief History of Time.* I took it home and put it on the table with a stack of other books that I had no intention of reading. Two days later, I gave it back to her and thanked her for letting me use it. I went to the library and found some nice general concepts but they were weak and high level. Three months later, we were sitting in her office talking about the four forces again (as I am consumed by them at this point) and she offered me her Stephen Hawking book again. I turned it down. I wasn't ready. Who wants to read a physics book? I avoided it by going the long way round, wearing garlic and crosses.

A week later, I went to talk to a doctor who lives in my neighborhood. He mentioned the Stephen Hawking book. "Year, yeah", I said, "but what about these four forces." I wanted answers but I didn't want to read, so, I stalled querying anyone who may know the answers to my mystery. No one had any idea what I was talking about. I realized that if it were that easy, I wouldn't be looking for the answer.

When I visited my mystical friend for the third time, she handed me the Stephen Hawking book. I didn't ask for it but it was beginning to become clear to me that I *had* to read it. I could no longer avoid it if I wanted to solve the mystery of the four forces in my dreams.

By the way, the Stephen Hawking book was neither difficult to read or understand. Two days after I began, I was acutely aware of what I needed to know and what to research further in my quest to understand atoms and the forces that act upon them so I could explain this behavioural construct.

The fact that many people have similar behaviour is not a new idea. How often have your heard, she acts just like her father or he acts just like his mother. School age children have a competitive silence. They don't reveal who they are to each other because they are just learning who they are, trying to fit into a mold that has been created for them. It is a simple task to pass someone by and make assumptions based on their outward appearance and by listening to the language of their environment. The natural tendencies in us are generally hidden from public view. They are reserved for our mates, close friends and irritating coworkers. It is often years later before the evidence of who we are becomes clear. It is written on our choices, decisions. And these are driven by the four forces within us.

The Universal Structure

A force pushes down or pulls upward. When you hang your jacket on a coat rack, the hook pulls upward on your jacket. If you place a quarter on your palm, the quarter pushes downward on your hand. These forces occur when one object touches another.

This wonderfully complex world of ours is a collection of molecules, which are made up of a number of atoms held together by electrons. The atom is comprised of a positively charged nucleus, electrons, protons and neutrons and each of these is comprised of even smaller particles. Living matter on earth is made up primarily of protons and neutrons. Every particle has an antiparticle, with which it can destroy. All things, comprising life are made up of these.

Spin

The molecules that effect living matter break down into smaller micro-particles and have a property called spin, which tells what the particle looks like from different directions. Picture a ball with a beautiful scene painted on it. A particle with the spin of 0 looks the same from every direction, like a dot. A particle with the spin of 1 looks one way when you look at one end but if you turn it 180º, it looks very different. A particle with spin 2 looks the same if you turn it half way around (180°) as at a full revolution (360°) or even smaller fractions like a hologram. Particles with a spin of ½ (such as the electron) must be turned completely around two times in order to know what it looks like in its entirety. It is spin that gives rise to forces between matter particles. Scientists have grouped the force-carrying particles into four categories according to their strength.

The Four Forces of the Universe

I have been arguing with myself about the relevance of these four forces for some time now. But they keep coming to me, in my dreams, when I look outside of my office window into nature and when I visit with my family. The conversations are considerably loud and full of energy for some, quiet, and thoughtful for others. So, I am compelled to describe the four hoping that their significance will become clear to you as you read on.

《》

There are literally hundreds of forces in the universe, but scientists have grouped them into four categories. They are the weak force, strong force, gravity and electromagnetism.

Table 4.1—Behaviour Model with Four Forces and Spin

Behaviour Model	Resolute Reality	Relative Reality	Stark Reality	Unreality
Ideals	Cause	Reality	Truth	Clairvoyance
The Body	Verbal	Physical	Mental	Spiritual
Ezekiel's Wheel	Man	Lion	Ox	Eagle
Profile	Philosopher	Warrior	Unifier	Mediator
Forces	Weak	Strong	Gravity	Electromagnetism
Spin Types	1 – Looks different from different directions. Looks the same at the 360° point like an arrow	1 – Looks different from different directions. Looks the same at the 360° point like an arrow	2 – looks the same if it is turned half a revolution – 180° degrees - double-headed arrow. Looks the same if turned through smaller fractions	½ - does not look the same if turned through one revolution. Must be turned through 2 complete revolutions
Spin Effect	Works on matter particles with spin ½	Works on matter particles with spin 1	Works on all matter particles.	Works on matter particles with spin 1

Gravity

Gravity is a long range, natural force of attraction exerted by a celestial body, (Earth) upon objects at or near its surface, (Moon). It draws in toward the center. This attraction exists between all objects. If you drop a quarter, it will fall to the ground, pulled down by the force of gravity. Gravity is a force that acts between objects even when they are not touching. Gravity is serious. How often have you changed your behaviour because someone gave you a look? It is the state of having weight, sobriety.

Sometimes forces, like gravity causes acceleration. It picks up momentum as it is being drawn down. This is similar to the effect that truth has. The more people who know and understand the truth, the better chance it has of acceptance. Truth changes things and its effect can be felt by the masses. Forces not only have magnitude but they also have direction. Down is the direction that gravity pulls. You may walk into a room, all high and happy. But if you pass too close to a serious person, they will surely pull you down into a more serious mood. Objects conform to gravity, just as gravity conforms to the objects they draw—no matter how powerful or weak.

Gravity waves roll right through everything (stars, galaxies, gas clouds, dust, planets and people) that occupies the universe. It is responsible for much of the structure of the universe. It is powerful in that it can bend light and change the perspective of the viewer, it can split the light so that it would seem that some of the light is taking a longer road. It is the force between two matter particles with spin-2, which looks the same no matter what direction you turn it. In other words, the person with gravity behaviour is most effective on others who possess the same perspective. Truth, like gravity does not seek to change your position. Truth stands on its own merit.

Just as gravity is always attractive, truth is grounding. It humbles. Truth quietly touches everything, unifying people. It looks at things, ideals, people from many different angles just as gravity waves bend light to change our perspective of the universe. Gravity and truth are constants—they look the same from every direction.

Electromagnetism

The force that gives materials their strength, their ability to bend, squeeze, stretch, or shatter, is the electromagnetic force. In humans, electromagnetism serves much the same purpose. The person exhibiting electromagnetism can touch another person and give them strength, advise them and take away their rigidity, hug them and raise their spirits, stretch their imagination or shatter their ego. Like grains of sand, it is the shape shifter—very difficult to pick out in a crowd.

This force results from a basic property of particles called electric charge. Charged particles at rest or in motion exert electric forces on each other. When charged, particles are in motion; they produce magnetic forces on each other. Electric and magnetic forces are both considered aspects of a single force, the electromagnetic force. It has the same function as gravity but on tiny sized particles instead of massive bodies. It is very strong compared to the gravitational force.

The resulting force of two positive charges is repulsive. The resulting force of two negative charges is also repulsive. But with electromagnetism, the result of a positive and a negative charge is attractive. In other words, the person with electromagnetic behaviour ignores those that are not in need of assistance. It goes directly to those that are in need of help (positive and negative situation or villain and victim). Electromagnetism works on virtually mass-less particles (people in need or who are under attack by a stronger entity). It affects particles with spin-1. I equate this to people with the strong force or weak force as the dominant force.

At high energy levels, (when a perceived injustice is being committed), electromagnetism gets stronger, more assertive, even aggressive. The instinctual drive to protect or defend emerges and then you may witness an attack that will bring silence to a crowded room. In this, individuals with electromagnetism as the dominant force all behave in the same manner. But when the energy begins to die down, and the highly charged person cools, they can become the mirror image of individuals around them—meeting needs, serving without complaint. In other words, at low energies, individuals with electromagnetism all look different. Stephen Hawking talks about the roulette wheel when describing particles with spin ½ such as those that carry the electromagnetic force.[11] He says, "the effect is rather like the behaviour of a roulette ball on a roulette wheel. At high energies (when the wheel is spun quickly) the ball behaves in essentially only one way—it rolls round and round getting stronger. But as the wheel slows, the energy of the ball decreases, and eventually the ball drops into one of the thirty-seven slots in the wheel. In other words, at low energies, we would think that there were thirty-seven different types of ball."

Strong Force

The strong force is less familiar because it is evident mainly over distances the size of the nucleus of an atom and its effects have not been observed. However, you have probably witnessed the strong force when you saw Elmer Fudd's head explode with anger on the Bugs Bunny cartoon.

The strong nuclear force holds the particles in the nucleus together, just as many company presidents and military leaders do over their subordinates. It is the strongest of the four forces—hundreds of times stronger than the electromagnetic force. But its range is shorter than gravity or electromagnetism. Much like a powerful lion that can run very fast but fizzles out quickly and has to rest.

Its range is much longer than the weak force but at high energies, the strong force becomes weaker. It acts as heavy-duty glue that keeps a

11 Stephen Hawking, A Brief History of Time, Bantam Books, a division of Random House, p. 74.

mass of particles together in the nucleus of an atom. This force is carried by spin-1 particles, which looks different at each end. It makes particles unstable since under its influence particles and antiparticles can destroy each other. It can be either repulsive (pushing protons apart if they come to near to each other) or attractive (pulling them together if they begin to drift too far apart).

The Weak Force

The fourth force is called the weak force. It is actually a form of the electromagnetic force, and is responsible for radioactivity and the decay processes. The tongue of the person with the weak force as a dominant behaviour acts in much the same way.

The weak force, which incidentally is not at all weak in the conventional view, is the source of engagement for short-range interactions. It acts only on matter particles with spin-½ such as those found in electromagnetism. In other words, there is a high probability that a war of words will happen between electromagnetism and the weak force if the weak force is engaged.

«»

Electricity and magnetism were unified into a single force in the 1870s. Recently, the electromagnetic force has been linked with the weak force. This suggests to physicists that all forces are different aspects of a single force. They have constructed theories called Grand Unification Theories (GUT) and Super-symmetric theories that try to demonstrate this unification. They have been able to link electromagnetic, weak and strong together but gravity still stands alone (the bear with three ribs in his mouth)[12]. This makes sense to me since

---

12 Daniel 7:1

clairvoyance, cause and reality are the three visible profiles that make up unreality in Ezekiel's wheel. Truth is hidden.

Truth like gravity still stands alone. So who will stand with truth? Who will uncover their eyes and see the truth? Gravity and electromagnetism see the world from opposite views—gravity takes in the whole picture and comes to know the pixels within it, electromagnetism sees one pixel at a time and combines them to create the whole picture. These two very different ideals amount to perspective. Perspective born of experience, which grew into truth. Perspective born of what has been read in a book and accepted as truth. In the course of normal human conflict, we assign labels to them—good and evil. But stepping back, what you really see is two victims who, for the moment, both happen to look like villains.

The Effect of Macromolecules on Human Behaviour

These four types with their four realities and purposes have repeated in a quaternal pattern since the beginning of time, as we know it. Just as the four forces have existed since the beginning. I know this to be true because man is a self-reproducing organism[13] and as in all self-reproducing organisms, there are constants that are passed from generation to generation just as there are variations that evolve due to natural selection.

Being self-reproducing means something else. It also means that the same gene in my genetic code that determines my dominant reality is the same gene in the

From now on, you (the serpent) and the woman will be enemies, and your offspring and her offspring will be enemies.

Genesis 3:15

---

13 Cairnes-Smith, Alexander Graham, (1991) Seven Clues to the Origin of Life: A Scientific Detective. Cambridge University Press

14 Genesis 3:1-24

lineage from which I descended. According to Bible history, there were four—Adam the man, Eve the woman, the serpent, and God. Adam the man had a penchant for words. He used them to name things, call attention to things, just as the philosopher does. Eve was curious, the investigator who went looking to fulfill her desires. The serpent sidled up beside her and offered her the most current truth and last, God exposed their sins and lies. But in His great empathy for them, He did not destroy them. He punished them instead.[14]

The four roles are indicative of Ezekiel's wheel. And in a conflict, the same types are pitted against each other to this day.

《》

Within living matter (humans) are macromolecules, which is a sort of cocktail of atoms, electrons and all of their components. These macromolecules reproduce themselves and are a part of the genetic code, which leads back to the first parents. They are also static and subject to the four forces of the universe—weak, strong, gravity and electromagnetism. These forces act on matter particles of which we are comprised. These forces give rise to and charge our emotions based on our thoughts.

Within and around the macromolecules are fast moving micro-particles, which have a tendency toward randomness[15]. Randomness is an efficient way for them to disperse energy as they crash into each other often at very high rates of speed. The randomness in micro-particles, combined with the environment, is what keeps us behaving as unique individuals instead of clones. The randomness, which point to differences in us, means that some are better able to adapt and cope as the world changes. The fine-tuning of our adaptation and coping skills mean we are able to lengthen our survival as a species. Each time we

---

15 Quantum Theory, Second Law of Thermodynamics

reproduce, our genetic strand becomes stronger and as the rulers of the earthly plane, hopefully we become more intelligent in our decisions and can teach each other.

《》

The whole of consciousness is reflected in a free-form dance of electrons somewhere in the mind of each person. Each emotion is a separate figure of the dance and is delivered with precision as the human brain toggles between limbic arousal (emotions, fight or flight, out of control, burnout) and cortical arousal (learning, creativity, problem solving, control and achievement).[16]

While every person comes complete with all four forces, which are activated when triggered by an event, it is the rise of the dominant team of forces (those we can see looking forward in Ezekiel's wheel) that determines how we act and interact most commonly with others. For some, the hidden force lies dormant until it is deliberately conjured up or summoned with a flight or fight condition. For others, the hidden force never surfaces.

Predestination or Freewill

For many years now, scientists have debated whether or not we behave as we do of our own freewill or if we are predestined to a course of action. For the scientist and clergy alike, it has been a moral issue, which points all the way to the question of whether or not God exists. Some sects have sought to suppress this type of research citing that the implications of such a study would be catastrophic to the church and the moral fiber of mankind. I disagree. Understanding the true nature of mankind will help him become what he must be to survive, to grow, to become better. Understanding is a bold step toward truth. Truth

---

16 Howard, Pierce. Owners Manual for the Brain

comes slowly, over time. An idea becomes true and remains true as long as the evidence points to it and continues to prove it. If either of these conditions fails, then we must find the truer answer.

People will always believe in God. God gives us hope. Without Him, what would be the point?

«»

On the issue of freewill and predestination, I say we have choices—choices to let the forces rise up or to suppress them, choices in our direction, choices to be neighborly or selfish. These are not determined by the macro factor. Even Ezekiel said, *"They (the wings) went in whatever direction the spirit chose."* These are determined by the randomness in our individual selves, the randomness of the microparticles within us.

And What of God?

Scientists and theologians, who have looked into the moral implications of predestination or determinism have dwelt on the worse case—that there is no God. Perhaps they were working at a too microscopic level or were facing their own fears and demons.

This construct was created first based on the evidence in the Bible and then from a scientific view. The Bible was written from visions, prophecies and histories of the time. And long before, the Greek philosophers (Plato) and the Eastern philosophers knew and understood what I know today.

I asked God to reveal Himself to me. He showed me truth in nature, goodness in those around me, and He gave me the ability to find the knowledge I desired. But, I am a diehard thinker, pushing the envelope and always, always digging deeper. I looked for logical conclusions and brighter gateways into truth. He touched my foot and when I shook the feel of electricity off He touched my neck and when I scratched my neck thinking it was a spider crawling there, He touched my hand. And I knew He was with me, guiding me. He led me to answers for questions I did not ask, questions I did not want to know the answers to. I am not a preacher or a prophet but He gave me a gift to interpret. I know he exists. I have no choice but to know. He speaks to me.

If you doubt this is true, just look for Him and no matter where you look, you will find Him. This may sound like religious rhetoric but it is the truth. He spoke to me in an ingenious way. He gave me the heart and words to write this book on a subject that I know little about, in a field not of my choosing. I think I know how Moses felt when he was chosen to ask Pharaoh to let the Jewish people go. Just like Moses, I know full well that many will not believe this, as it is not in their nature. Then I look back at Romans 8:30 and I weep for them. Were they not also chosen for some important work in God's plan?

In the spiritual sense of the creation around us, in the expression of art and beauty, in our yearning towards God, the soul expands upward and finds the fulfillment of something implanted in it's nature. The authorization for this development is within us. It is a striving born within our consciousness. It is an inner light proceeding from a greater power than ours.

Now, when I look at the treetops from my second story office window, as the energy from the sun is dissipating over this side of creation, my heart becomes full. I shake my head in disbelief. God is still with us, watching and taking care.

FOUR

Making Sense of the World

Give thanks to the Lord, for he is good. Give thanks to the God
of gods. Give thanks to the Lord of lords: to him who alone does
great wonders, who by his understanding made the heavens,
who spread out the earth upon the waters, who made the great
lights—the sun to govern the day, the moon and stars to govern
the night; His love endures forever

Psalm 136:1-9

We live by laws—but as human nature dictates to us, we break them
as often as we can—if they conflict with the reality coded in our genes,
if they don't make practical sense, if they don't allow us to fulfill our
encoded destiny. This is how laws are changed or exclusions for laws are
written.

There is a high probability that a causal scheme exists at the base of
atomic phenomena just as it is the root of conflict that continues to
plague mankind. Through this causal scheme, we can predict the events
of the future and determine the truth needed for change. Change will
lead us to survival.

This book is concerned not with the individual behaviour but with the average behavior of mankind. Human life is proverbially uncertain. The next quantum jump of an atom is as uncertain as your life or mine. Averages are predictable because they are averages. So, which action will we take next? It is inconceivable that an atom can be so evenly balanced between two alternative courses that it can go either way. There must be somewhere, the ultimate deciding factor. This is an appeal for more knowledge, wisdom and intuition.

Everything we do or decide to do from this point forward depends on an act of volition of which we have no knowledge. There is a thought being generated in man that will cause the next war or begin our quest for peace.

The continuation of life is dependent on the surrounding elements and therefore must be looked at macroscopically—from the viewpoint of the needs of many. Forget about races, they have no bearing. It is not about black or white. Forget about gender, it has no bearing. Forget about age, even the youngest has a viewpoint and a creative nature. Forget about education—the less educated may have more to offer because they have not be restricted by the orthodox, conventional view. The enemy looks like me; the victim looks like me, the liberator looks like me, the defender looks like me. We were not meant to know the difference between these four by looking at the outside. It is coded in actions, words and deeds.

As for the atom and the universe, I believe that behind all of the research and conclusions that there is a backdrop contiguous with the backdrop in the brain. The spontaneous behaviour of the atom sparks a decision, just as our causal behaviour (thoughts) becomes the root of the reason. Cause, in the decision of the atom, has something in common with the cause of the decision made in the brain. We must give the mind the power to decide the behavior of the atoms individually—in fact to tamper with the odds on atomic behaviour. This is called choice, freewill. We are never giving up the freedom of the mind and will.

The unity of man's consciousness into the four beings of Ezekiel's wheel is not an illusion. It is not my dream alone. Consider the collective behaviour. We are all four and all four exist in us. We are aware of all four. We must open up our minds so that our future generations can be susceptible to all four and then…there can be peace.

There are no final and absolute values when it comes to human behavior. There is a divine element in man's nature waiting to be awakened by a touch, an imperceptible noise or a sign.

Epilogue

Okay, I admit that babies being born in a recurring theme of these four profiles seem a bit hard to swallow, unbelievable, even unthinkable. I wrestled with the idea myself as I was researching this construct. Everything I know and believe about individuality and my unique self came into question. If this is all true, *am I special?*

Yet, I cannot deny the evidence—the interviews, the observations, the situational analysis, the biographies of those in the past. When the forces rise up, there are very specific reactions that occur. The difference between people is a matter of degree. This degree is the equivalent of wisdom, which has nothing to do with what I look like on the outside.

But again, an idea like this one comes to be true. It is not true because I wrote this book. This idea has been around for centuries. Asian cultures have depended on the knowledge of these recurring profiles to improve relationships among themselves. This is apparent in divorce statistics and business relationships of the past. They have come to understand the code.

Our minds are connected to the world. It creates what we see. Our minds, indeed, define the world as we strive for some level of perfection. The thoughts that we have—the beautiful and the sullen—and our even deeper feelings like hatred and prejudice are part of a collective consciousness, which passes from person to person. When we create fear in our minds, the world predictably becomes a fearful place, a cruel place to hide from. We begin to shrink in statue. When we create a nurturing place to be valued, the world is not threatening and everything we desire is attainable. We become more desirable. Seeing the world as nurturing is an exercise in diligence. When I think negative thoughts, the world looks gray and awful. When I see the truth of life represented by positive ideas, the world around me seems to be influenced by them and falls right in line.

It is our dominant reality working with the second and third, trying to find the hidden. It is the forces within us, rising up when signaled. We are bound together and held tightly thinking we are different. But we are the same as long as something in me can connect with something in you.

The human psyche is a wheel, spinning forward to gain knowledge, looking backward and forcing the issues of our lives. Rolling in the direction of cause, and with cooperation, we gain in strength. It is the normal growth cycle. In the opposite direction, the direction of truth, there is conflict, emotional frustration, persecution and even war. We brush the gnats away with our tails and then we grow in wisdom and begin to adapt and change. Daniel's vision in which the bear stands with the three ribs in his mouth eating his fill comes to mind. Then the one with the iron jaw comes to rule by the force of his will and crushes the truth. And after he rules and his life is extinguished, then can there be peace?

Can we get off this wheel? Who knows? I like to think that if we know and learn to recognize the rise of the four forces before they take over our brains and actions, flight or fight, then we can begin to change how they affect us. We can adapt unlike the species who have died out. In time, our children's children may act differently.

One thing is certain, we must unify the four somehow. The Grand Unification Theory, if it is ever fully developed, may help to align us. But without truth, gravity in the mix, there can be no peace. Look in nature. Nature is truth. It is our example for harmony and beauty. The beauty in nature has the power to transform the heart of a man.

Am I special? Of course. I am special to those who love me. I am a totally unique individual. I am special because I am God's child and I know how much he loves me.

Appendix

About the Author

Connie J. Allen is an internationally recognized speaker and organizational strategist whose expertise is facilitating problem-solving teams. Her understanding of the business environment has led to three prior books—Intuitive Power: Experience and Applications, Coded Messages: Solving the Mystery in Work Relationships and The Psychology of Customer Service Excellence: Human Strategies for Front Line Leaders. She is the founder and managing director of LUCIDITY *A Human Performance Improvement Company*.

She resides in Houston, Texas with her son Thaddeus and daughter Lauren.

info@callen&associates.com

Select Bibliography

Albert, D. Z., (1992). *Quantum Mechanics and Experience*, Cambridge, Mass.

Bell, J. S. (1987). *Speakable and Unspeakable in Quantum Mechanics*, Cambridge

Capra, Fritjof, (1991). *The Tao of Physics*, Shambhala Publications, Inc.

Easton, M.G., M.A, D.D., (1897). *Illustrated Bible Dictionary*, Third Edition, Thomas Nelson

Eccles, J. C. and Popper, K. R., (1977). *The Self and Its Brain*, Berlin

Eddington, Sir Arthur Stanley, (1928). *The Nature of the Physical World*, Macmillan Company

Fielder, David, (1961). *Ancient Cosmology and Early Christian Symbolism*, Quest Books

Hawking, Stephen W., (1988). *A Brief History of Time*, Bantam

Honderich, T. A., (1988). *Theory of Determinism: The Mind, Neuro-science, and Life-Hopes*, Oxford

Howard, Pierce J., Ph.D., (2000). *The Owner's Manual for the Brain*, Bard Press

Jung, C. G., (1938). *Psychology and Religion*, Yale University Press

Kohl, Herbert, (1992). *From Archetype to Zeitgeist*, Little Brown and Company. Boston, Toronto, London

Lambert, Frank L. Professor Emeritus, (2000). *The Second Law of Thermodynamics*, Occidental College, Los Angeles, CA 90041 www.secondlaw.com

McGreal, Ian P., Editor, (1995). *Great Thinkers of the Eastern World*, HarperCollins

Oxford University Press, (1995). *The Oxford Companion to Philosophy*

Paul W. Zitzewitz, Mark Davies, Robert F. Neff, (1992). *Physics Principles and Problems*, McMillan/McGraw Hill

Shroyer, Jo Ann, (1993). *Quarks, Critters and Chaos—What Science Terms Really Mean*, Prentice Hall

Tyndale House Publishers, Holy Bible, New Living Translation, 1996. www.tyndale.com

Wolfram Research. www.wolfram.com, Lunar Calendar Verification

Zondervan Publishing House. (1984). *Serendipity Bible New International Version*

Some Questions I Have Been Asked

1. Who are the characters in the story?

Jacob represents the weak force, which is words—cutting and critical. It goes in one direction. Seraph is electromagnetism, which defends the innocent and the guilty alike. She seeks knowledge from Jacob, who she sees before her and from Solon who is behind her in the circle. Electromagnetism (social conscience) goes both ways. Grace is the strong force, whose outbursts defy intelligence and yet she is very intelligent, the Renaissance woman, capable of accomplishing anything. The strong force drives the direction of the spin, simply because she is so strong and carried by momentum. The strong force is frequently the reason why the world goes off course. It sometimes takes a while for Grace to recognize the truth. In the meantime, an awful lot of damage has been done. Solon represents gravity, truth. It flows through all of us and keeps us grounded.

2. What are the symbols at the beginning of each segment in the story?

The symbols are polyhedrons. Plato described the elemental continuum of which the world is comprised as fire, air, earth and water. Fire, which represents blood, is a collection of charged particles, something molded as in man. The tetrahedron (four sided pyramid) symbolizes fire. The octahedron is air, a solid bounded by eight plane faces. It is two pyramids, adhered at the base. Earth is a solid represented by a cube with six faces all equal. The icosahedron is the most complex with twenty faces and represents water. It can extinguish fire and change the composition of air and earth.

3. Which of the four represents God?

None of the four children represent God. God, if he chooses to be in this story at all, would be represented by the father.

4. Why were the names Jacob, Seraph, Grace and Solon chosen for the illustration?

They were chosen for their meaning. Jacob is a Hebrew name which means supplanter—one who wrongfully or illegally seizes and holds the place of another. Seraph literally means angel and Solon means sage. In the dictionary, Grace means many things including unmerited divine assistance, approval and favor. These are obviously symbolic of their roles.

5. How do I use this information?

How we choose to live, think or be is entirely up to each individual. Reach for your own conclusions. We will meet somewhere in the middle.

Gregorian Translation of the Lunar Calendar

	From				To		Profile
2	1	1851	-	2	19	1852	Philosopher
2	20	1852	-	2	7	1853	Warrior
2	8	1853	-	1	28	1854	Unifier
1	29	1854	-	2	16	1855	Mediator
2	17	1855	-	2	5	1856	Philosopher
2	6	1856	-	1	25	1857	Warrior
1	26	1857	-	2	13	1858	Unifier
2	14	1858	-	2	2	1859	Mediator
2	3	1859	-	1	22	1860	Philosopher
1	23	1860	-	2	9	1861	Warrior
2	10	1861	-	1	29	1862	Unifier
1	30	1862	-	2	17	1863	Mediator
2	18	1863	-	2	7	1864	Philosopher
2	8	1864	-	1	26	1865	Warrior
1	27	1865	-	2	14	1866	Unifier
2	15	1866	-	2	4	1867	Mediator
2	5	1867	-	1	24	1868	Philosopher
1	25	1868	-	2	10	1869	Warrior

2	11	1869	-	1	30	1870	Unifier
1	31	1870	-	2	18	1871	Mediator
2	19	1871	-	2	8	1872	Philosopher
2	9	1872	-	1	28	1873	Warrior
1	29	1873	-	2	16	1874	Unifier
2	17	1874	-	2	5	1875	Mediator
2	6	1875	-	1	25	1876	Philosopher
1	26	1876	-	2	12	1877	Warrior
2	13	1877	-	2	1	1878	Unifier
2	2	1878	-	1	21	1879	Mediator
1	22	1879	-	2	9	1880	Philosopher
2	10	1880	-	1	29	1881	Warrior
1	30	1881	-	2	17	1882	Unifier
2	18	1882	-	2	7	1883	Mediator
2	8	1883	-	1	27	1884	Philosopher
1	28	1884	-	2	14	1885	Warrior
2	15	1885	-	2	3	1886	Unifier
2	4	1886	-	1	23	1887	Mediator
1	24	1887	-	2	11	1888	Philosopher
2	12	1888	-	1	30	1889	Warrior
1	31	1889	-	1	20	1890	Unifier
1	21	1890	-	2	8	1891	Mediator
2	9	1891	-	1	29	1892	Philosopher
1	30	1892	-	2	16	1893	Warrior
2	17	1893	-	2	5	1894	Unifier
2	6	1894	-	1	25	1895	Mediator
1	26	1895	-	2	12	1896	Philosopher
2	13	1896	-	2	1	1897	Warrior

2	2	1897	-	1	21	1898	Unifier
1	22	1898	-	2	9	1899	Mediator
2	10	1899	-	1	30	1900	Philosopher
1	31	1900	-	2	18	1901	Warrior
2	19	1901	-	2	7	1902	Unifier
2	8	1902	-	1	28	1903	Mediator
1	29	1903	-	2	15	1904	Philosopher
2	16	1904	-	2	3	1905	Warrior
2	4	1905	-	1	24	1906	Unifier
1	25	1906	-	2	12	1907	Mediator
2	13	1907	-	2	1	1908	Philosopher
2	2	1908	-	1	21	1909	Warrior
1	22	1909	-	2	9	1910	Unifier
2	10	1910	-	1	29	1911	Mediator
1	30	1911	-	2	17	1912	Philosopher
2	18	1912	-	2	5	1913	Warrior
2	6	1913	-	1	25	1914	Unifier
1	26	1914	-	2	13	1915	Mediator
2	14	1915	-	2	2	1916	Philosopher
2	3	1916	-	1	22	1917	Warrior
1	23	1917	-	2	10	1918	Unifier
2	11	1918	-	2	0	1919	Mediator
2	1	1919	-	2	19	1920	Philosopher
2	20	1920	-	2	7	1921	Warrior
2	8	1921	-	1	27	1922	Unifier
1	28	1922	-	2	15	1923	Mediator
2	16	1923	-	2	4	1924	Philosopher
2	5	1924	-	1	23	1925	Warrior

1	24	1925	-	2	12	1926	Unifier
2	13	1926	-	2	1	1927	Mediator
2	2	1927	-	1	22	1928	Philosopher
1	23	1928	-	2	9	1929	Warrior
2	10	1929	-	1	29	1930	Unifier
1	30	1930	-	2	16	1931	Mediator
2	17	1931	-	2	5	1932	Philosopher
2	6	1932	-	1	25	1933	Warrior
1	26	1933	-	2	13	1934	Unifier
2	14	1934	-	2	3	1935	Mediator
2	4	1935	-	1	23	1936	Philosopher
1	24	1936	-	2	10	1937	Warrior
2	11	1937	-	1	30	1938	Unifier
1	31	1938	-	2	18	1939	Mediator
2	19	1939	-	2	7	1940	Philosopher
2	8	1940	-	1	26	1941	Warrior
1	27	1941	-	2	14	1942	Unifier
2	15	1942	-	2	4	1943	Mediator
2	5	1943	-	1	24	1944	Philosopher
1	25	1944	-	2	12	1945	Warrior
2	13	1945	-	2	1	1946	Unifier
2	2	1946	-	1	21	1947	Mediator
1	22	1947	-	2	9	1948	Philosopher
2	10	1948	-	1	28	1949	Warrior
1	29	1949	-	2	16	1950	Unifier
2	17	1950	-	2	5	1951	Mediator
2	6	1951	-	1	26	1952	Philosopher
1	27	1952	-	2	13	1953	Warrior

2	14	1953	-	2	2	1954	Unifier
2	3	1954	-	1	23	1955	Mediator
1	24	1955	-	2	11	1956	Philosopher
2	12	1956	-	1	30	1957	Warrior
1	31	1957	-	2	17	1958	Unifier
2	18	1958	-	2	7	1959	Mediator
2	8	1959	-	1	27	1960	Philosopher
1	28	1960	-	2	14	1961	Warrior
2	15	1961	-	2	4	1962	Unifier
2	5	1962	-	1	24	1963	Mediator
1	25	1963	-	2	12	1964	Philosopher
2	13	1964	-	2	1	1965	Warrior
2	2	1965	-	1	20	1966	Unifier
1	21	1966	-	2	8	1967	Mediator
2	9	1967	-	1	29	1968	Philosopher
1	30	1968	-	2	16	1969	Warrior
2	17	1969	-	2	5	1970	Unifier
2	6	1970	-	1	26	1971	Mediator
1	27	1971	-	2	14	1972	Philosopher
2	15	1972	-	2	2	1973	Warrior
2	3	1973	-	1	22	1974	Unifier
1	23	1974	-	2	10	1975	Mediator
2	11	1975	-	1	30	1976	Philosopher
1	31	1976	-	2	17	1977	Warrior
2	18	1977	-	2	6	1978	Unifier
2	7	1978	-	1	27	1979	Mediator
1	28	1979	-	2	15	1980	Philosopher
2	16	1980	-	2	4	1981	Warrior

2	5	1981	-	1	24	1982	Unifier
1	25	1982	-	2	12	1983	Mediator
2	13	1983	-	2	1	1984	Philosopher
2	2	1984	-	2	19	1985	Warrior
2	20	1985	-	2	8	1986	Unifier
2	9	1986	-	1	28	1987	Mediator
1	29	1987	-	2	16	1988	Philosopher
2	17	1988	-	2	5	1989	Warrior
2	6	1989	-	1	26	1990	Unifier
1	27	1990	-	2	14	1991	Mediator
2	15	1991	-	2	3	1992	Philosopher
2	4	1992	-	1	22	1993	Warrior
1	23	1993	-	2	9	1994	Unifier
2	10	1994	-	1	30	1995	Mediator
1	31	1995	-	2	18	1996	Philosopher
2	19	1996	-	2	6	1997	Warrior
2	7	1997	-	1	27	1998	Unifier
1	28	1998	-	2	15	1999	Mediator
2	16	1999	-	2	4	2000	Philosopher
2	5	2000	-	1	23	2001	Warrior
1	24	2001	-	2	11	2002	Unifier
2	12	2002	-	2	0	2003	Mediator
2	1	2003	-	1	21	2004	Philosopher
1	22	2004	-	2	8	2005	Warrior
2	9	2005	-	1	28	2006	Unifier
1	29	2006	-	2	17	2007	Mediator
2	18	2007	-	2	6	2008	Philosopher
2	7	2008	-	1	25	2009	Warrior

1	26	2009	-	2	13	2010	Unifier
2	14	2010	-	2	2	2011	Mediator
2	3	2011	-	1	22	2012	Philosopher
1	23	2012	-	2	9	2013	Warrior
2	10	2013	-	1	30	2014	Unifier
1	31	2014	-	2	18	2015	Mediator
2	19	2015	-	2	7	2016	Philosopher
2	8	2016	-	1	27	2017	Warrior
1	28	2017	-	2	15	2018	Unifier
2	16	2018	-	2	4	2019	Mediator
2	5	2019	-	1	24	2020	Philosopher
1	25	2020	-	2	11	2021	Warrior
2	12	2021	-	2	0	2022	Unifier
2	1	2022	-	1	21	2023	Mediator
1	22	2023	-	2	9	2024	Philosopher
2	10	2024	-	1	28	2025	Warrior
1	29	2025	-	2	16	2026	Unifier
2	17	2026	-	2	5	2027	Mediator
2	6	2027	-	1	25	2028	Philosopher
1	26	2028	-	2	12	2029	Warrior
2	13	2029	-	2	2	2030	Unifier
2	3	2030	-	1	22	2031	Mediator

0-595-21617-X

www.ingramcontent.com/pod-product-compliance
Lightning Source LLC
Chambersburg PA
CBHW061305280526
45784CB00002B/896